# RUNNING
# IN THE RAIN

Seriously... How Hard Can it Be?

## EFFECTIVE STRATEGIES FOR
## CREATING A MORE PRODUCTIVE
## AND FULFILLING LIFE

by
**PAUL WESTON**

**RUNNING IN THE RAIN** – *Seriously… How Hard Can it Be?*
*Effective Strategies for Creating a More Productive and Fulfilling Life*

Paperback Book ISBN: 978-1-953806-17-8
Ebook ISBN: ISBN: 978-1-953806-18-5

Published by Spotlight Publishing™

Cover Design: Angie Analya
Cover Background Image: Adobe Stock
Interior Design: Soumi Goswami

Spotlight Publishing™ https://SpotlightPublishing.pro

Copies of this book may be ordered directly from
https://www.andrewjane.com/running-in-the-rain

We invite you to submit reviews of this book.
To contact Paul Weston:
Email: paulweston@andrewjane.com
Phone: 905.407.7963

https://www.andrewjane.com/

# RUNNING
# IN THE RAIN

Seriously... How Hard Can it Be?

EFFECTIVE STRATEGIES FOR
CREATING A MORE PRODUCTIVE
AND FULFILLING LIFE

by
## PAUL WESTON

Spotlight PUBLISHING
Goodyear, AZ

# Table of Contents

*For Mum, Dad and Katie.*

# Foreword

Lieutenant-General Sir Robert Fulton KBE
*former Commandant General Royal Marines,*
*Deputy Chief of the Defence Staff (UK) and Governor of Gibraltar*
Chief Executive Officer, Global Leadership Foundation

From the first page, Paul Weston leaves his readers in no doubt about the ending he aims to reach. '*Running in the Rain*' is a book that is both intensely personal and engagingly open, drawing us into his world, while strongly encouraging each of us to draw on, and build on, his experiences and his methods to achieve our own potential. He wants us to create for ourselves, in his words, "*a more productive and fulfilling life*" in all its aspects: professional, personal and social. While the title, as a metaphor for life itself, might appear to relate only to those committed to hard physical exercise in unpleasant conditions, the ideas expressed here are relevant to all aspects of our daily existence as we move through life and deal with its vicissitudes.

The training and experiences of Paul's 26-year career in the Royal Marines have clearly framed much of his approach and yet the fundamental philosophy of his parents shines through, while the lessons of a successful second career in business provide the balance and the polish. The Royal Marines taught him the military version of the values of courage, determination, unselfishness and integrity – yet the roots of all of those were clearly already present and, as this book shows, they play a significant part in his approach to his professional, personal and social life today.

Excellence is a habit, and the pursuit, development and maintenance of that habit is a consistent theme as the bedrock of success in any activity or venture. All who have acquired that habit understand very clearly that they have done so through practising and maintaining their focus on whatever they are trying to achieve. The acquisition of expertise requires that focus, underlining the critical importance of the mind as the driving force in achieving our potential.

Goals are, traditionally, the foundation of organisational and personal intent to improve. Many will therefore be surprised at the arresting statement that '*Goals Stink*', and yet there are a number of vivid examples here of goals that have not only failed to achieve their objective but have actually proved to be regressive. Having adroitly focussed our attention, he explains that it is goals in isolation that stink. Goals on their own are, at best, an opportunity for a temporary injection of '*feel good*' and, at worst, a stick with which to continually beat ourselves or our teams. Even the application of the widely acknowledged SMART acronym does not, of itself, acquit goals of the charge. Yet, if we stand back for a moment, it is clear to us that goals are indeed meaningless, or worse, unless they are set in the context of continuous performance analysis and are consistently aimed at steady improvement. That context is built on the systems and routines that frame the activity in question, whether sales targets, weight loss or race times.

The framework of any such context is the plan – whether personal, team or corporate, whether civilian or military. Planning is an essential activity but, as Paul identifies, it is not always conducted with the rigour that it deserves. Its formality may vary depending on the nature of the task and the number of participants, but we cannot achieve our true potential without it. We need to know the objectives, the deadlines, the actors, and what assumptions we can make about, for example, other activities that may have happened beforehand or that may be going on at the same time.

In the military world, we recognise that no plan survives contact with the enemy and hence, it is the conduct of the planning process that matters more than the plan that has emerged. In addition to the plan, we must assess the enemy's likely actions and reactions and make sure that we have alternative plans and follow-on plans. Similarly, we must prepare, not only for the resistance we expect, but also for tougher resistance in some places and weaker resistance in others, and we must not allow that to distort the cohesion of the plan. We must also be prepared to adjust timings and objectives to take account of changing circumstances. Here of course lies one potential divergence – what is fixed and what can be changed? If we are preparing for one of Paul's Ironman triathlons, the deadline (i.e., the start date and time) cannot be changed – at least not by us. If, however, we are planning the D Day invasion of Europe in June 1944, the weather has a 'vote' and the exact date of D Day may be amenable to some change until quite close to the event itself. The key is, as ever, the judgement on such issues early in the planning process so that, in working back to the start point, we can take account of all the constraints and possibilities.

Planning for an activity in which we are the only participant is, of course, simpler than planning for one in which there are many. While it may be simpler, it is perhaps harder in one crucial respect: we have to overcome our own reluctance, especially if it is metaphorically raining outside. Organisations, teams, and groups embarking on such a venture have the advantage of mutual support, provided that they can communicate effectively.

The military world is not alone in depending on communication as one of the key factors for successful operations. Any organisation or activity in which teams or multiple individuals have a part to play must make sure that all components know what they must do. To the military, the critical importance of such communication has, for a long time, ensured that the preparation for any operation, large or small, is a comparatively formal affair with briefings and, when possible, rehearsals to ensure that everyone involved, at every level, can answer the questions: *"What is my commander's intention?'* and *"What is my part in it?'* If translated to the civilian world, could we say that everyone, at every level, understands their boss's intention and their own contribution to it? Without such coherence, individuals will find it hard to focus and the output of the team will be blurred. In the modern era, the means of communication have multiplied many times and now include all forms of social media in addition to the traditional, structured methods whose receipt, dispatch and existence were formally recorded in files. As a result, there is now an even greater need for positive co-ordination and good discipline – the habits of excellence.

Now that we have the plan to achieve our objectives (our goals) as well as the systems and routines that provide the context within which we will prepare for, and meet, those objectives, only one thing remains: *Just Get on With It.* Planning is an essential part of this whole process, but we must always remember that there comes a moment when the analysis stops, and the action starts. *How hard can it be?* We know all about adversity - how hard it might be - from our analysis of the tasks required, but we will never really know until we start – so let's get going!

Adversity takes many forms and Paul analyses the range of such issues in searingly honest detail. *How hard can it be?* For each person, the answer to that question will differ. It is also true that the answer to that question is known only to each person – and each person's potential will be different. Some adversities are visible or widely recognised, but most lie hidden within each one of us. Only we can guess at our true potential and yet, armed with the approaches set out in *Running in the Rain*, we all have the capacity to surprise ourselves. Napoleon is reported to have said that the mental is to the physical as three is to one; here we see the interconnections between the mental and the physical, and the dependence of each on the other.

Paul has written a book not only to inspire us to get out and get things done, but also to give us a framework that we can use for our own circumstances. Paul's experience and expertise are as wide as anyone could imagine and he draws on it all – military, business, musical (Seriously - who else would be able to run John Williams's '*Summon the Heroes*' in his/her head in the last hour of a triathlon? Most of us at least need some words to sing). Here we can start to see not only what we might achieve for ourselves but also, and more importantly, how we can tackle it. *Seriously – How Hard Can It Be?*

**Robert Fulton**
December 2020

The more I read of this immensely enjoyable book the more blessed I felt – why? because I was reminded how fortunate I am to work in an environment where I am surrounded by individuals who snatch every opportunity to '*run in the rain*'. Working with those who have incurred life-changing injuries resulting in paralysis and limb loss but who have positively reconfigured their lives and grasped the future is deeply humbling but also unsettling – do I approach my life with the same positive mindset? In a similar vein, Paul Weston prompts us to ask ourselves whether we are maximising life's opportunities, and he presents a framework and a practical set of tools to help us both recognise and realise our potential. He achieves this through a richness of story-telling made possible by the fullness of his own life experiences – son, husband, Royal Marine, athlete, musician, businessman. Here is someone we want to listen to and who we want to learn from as he presents us with an invaluable guide to understanding our personal and professional selves and how we can maximise the gift of life.

— **David Pond**
Chief Executive,
Great Britain Wheelchair Rugby

Paul has written a book not only to inspire us to get out and get things done, but also to give us a framework that we can use for our own circumstances. His experience and expertise are as wide as anyone could imagine and he draws on it all.

— **Sir Robert Fulton**
former Commandant General Royal Marines

As an avid reader rarely do I read a book that seamlessly integrates personal and professional lessons one chapter at a time. Through Paul's unique experiences, *"Running in the Rain"* exceptionally helps elevate your best self to the next level with simple, yet crucial tools that will make the most arduous of tasks pale in comparison to the feeling of true fulfilment once achieved. Bravo Paul!

**— Gisela Carere**
President, Benchmark Benefit Solutions Inc

*"Running in the Rain"* offers the reader a wealth of pragmatic, relevant, and easy to follow steps to enhance every aspect of professional and personal life. This seminal book is a treasure trove of practical advice and a must read for the leaders of today and tomorrow. Paul's writing is authentic and engaging while it points you on a clear path to greater fulfilment and success. I wish I had read this 20 years ago!

**— Cheryl McClellan**
Chief Operations Officer, The Arthritis Society

*"Running in the Rain"* is an excellent and practical *'how-to'* guide for any person who wants to accomplish more in all aspects of their life. Systems, strategies and resilience matter and this book is full of clearly presented information and examples to help create a purposeful life and *'get things done'*.

**— Cliff Trollope**
Lieutenant Colonel (retired) and Partner,
Enterprise Risk Services, MNP LLP

*"Running in the Rain"* had me engrossed from page one. Paul writes in a manner that feels like he is having a candid conversation with you. This book will have you look at how busy you truly areas well as why the 'to do list' may be holding you back. It is a much-needed and highly-recommended read in today's hectic *'always-on'* society.

**— Paolina Allan**
Former Professional Triathlete,
Top-Ranked Masters Road Cyclist.

# Introduction

*T*his isn't a book about running. Neither is it a book about the weather. So, if you found it in the meteorologist athlete section, it has been misplaced. Where should it be then? Maybe you could decide because I'm not certain either. So, let me explain.

I have always thought that *Running in the Rain* was a metaphor for life. The running part is synonymous with the idea that we are constantly moving forward from the moment we are born until the day we die. We move physically from place to place. We move educationally through the information we gather each day. We move emotionally, spiritually, in our relationships and in our careers. It doesn't have to be far, but we all move somewhere every day.

And we all do it at different speeds, just like running. If you are actually into running, you'll recognize there are times when you *want* to go for a run, you know you *need* to go for a run, but you don't because... well, just because...

Even if you aren't a runner, maybe you would like to try it and get into it to the point where you might enter a short race and see how it goes. See? You are starting to move forward a bit faster now. But using running as a metaphor, again, maybe it isn't actually running you want to get into. Maybe you want a new career, or a new house, or a new relationship or you want to just do things better and make some improvements in your life. But there always seems to be something stopping you.

Let's consider the rain part, then. Who wants to run in the rain? Well, I'm totally fine with it, although I know many who aren't. In fact, even a dark cloud in the sky is enough to put some people off the idea.

But running in the rain is really just a metaphor for all the things that stand in the way of us moving forward in life. You could tell me there are a whole host of very good reasons why you aren't doing these things, which is the same as telling me the reason you can't go for a run is that it is raining. I find there is a word that fits quite well with all these "reasons" – in fact, it usually replaces that word: *excuses*.

In life, we waste time finding reasons not to do something we know we *want* to do, something we know we *need* to do and something we know isn't really too bad. And so we just don't do it. Or, when we do get around to doing it, we don't do it well or we fall short of our expectations and go on to feel pretty lousy about it. That's rather like not running very fast because it's raining. Or not running as far as you really should because it's raining. Or not even getting out of the door to go running… because it's raining.

I was lucky that I grew up as an only child in a disciplined household. My parents were loving people who wanted me to have the very best opportunities in life and I think I can say they achieved that because, looking back, there aren't many things I would change.

Of all the disciplines they passed on to me, probably the most valuable was the ability to get things done. My mother's mantra was always – *never leave to tomorrow what you can do today* and anyone who knows me would probably agree this is really part of my DNA. In fact, I have been accused of behaving somewhat obsessively about being functional, but I am more interested in living an easy life by being efficient than anything else. Likewise, I have a natural aversion to wasting my time and energy on activities that are not practical or do not serve a useful purpose (and no, I am really not very patient with people who dither around rather than getting on with stuff).

Over the years I have watched people spread their energy in so many different directions they barely succeed in getting anything done in any area of their life. I see them become obsessed with goals and yet they usually fail to achieve any of them. They are barely able to focus on a task for more than a few minutes, they live in a world of total distraction and they are dominated by email, chat, and social media; they procrastinate and then sink into a generally self-inflicted world of adversity. And this is what drove me to write this book... well, that and hearing quite a few people who know me actually saying, "you should write a book about being efficient and getting on with things you want to do."

Is this a book about time management? Not really, because I don't think you can manage time, all you can do is focus on how much energy you put into things in order to master and take control of that time.

Is it supposed to be motivational? I wouldn't class myself as a motivational speaker or writer. Both my parents are still alive, and I haven't lost a limb or had to recover from cancer, so I don't really have a story that qualifies. But for me, motivation is a willingness to act, and that is really defined by the environment in which we place ourselves. So, if this book helps you create the right environment, then great.

Is it a book about self-help? Well, I hope whoever reads it finds it useful and tries some of the systems enclosed within its pages because they all work for me, and they also seem to work for pretty much all the people I have shared them with through my programs over the years. But you can be the judge of that.

So, what *are* we going to get into? The short answer is, plenty of effective strategies for creating a more productive and fulfilling life, both at the office and in our personal world!

I believe we spend every second of our lives in one of three Energy Zones: Professional (doing stuff that makes us money), Personal (doing stuff for ourselves), and Social (doing stuff with our friends and family). And I also believe that if we try to dilute them by putting them all together (and most people do – for too much of their time), we don't do any of them very well, and we usually feel bad about it. So, this book explores that concept in great detail.

We will also look at how our physical activity – and working hard – actually replenishes our Mental Energy pack. Ever done something that made you tired, but also stimulated you – like going for a run? Good, let's see if we can do more of that.

We'll consider how goals have been letting us down for years and how focusing on *a system* is a much more valuable way for us to be successful at pretty much anything we do.

Are you focusing on doing the right stuff and, if so, how do you know?

How much of your life is dominated by communication and distraction? Probably too much, so let's look at a system to help with that.

If going for a metaphorical run seems like it would take too much effort, then you are probably making an excuse and your perception – particularly of the effort required – needs to change.

Have you been avoiding tasks you know you should be doing – like going for a run when it's raining? Well, we are going to have a good look at that as well.

And, finally, if you think *Running in the Rain* is a good example of overcoming adversity, then we are starting to talk the same language because this whole book is designed to help anyone who needs a bit of encouragement to get out there in the wet and get it done, and we will have a look at what adversity looks like for many people.

When we *run* in the *rain*, we take on more of a challenge than we do by not running at all, or by only running when the sun is out. We look the adversity of those raindrops straight in the face and decide they may make us a little uncomfortable, and running through them may not be pleasant, but it means that YOU rule your destiny, your direction and how far YOU will go. And the rain will not stop you.

Anyway, if you think you know in which section of the store, library or online outlet this book should be stationed, then maybe you could put it there. Or maybe you could just keep reading. And, if you do, then I hope you discover some great tools that help you feel good about many aspects of your life. If you are in doubt, picture this scene: you want to go for a run and you put your running clothes and shoes on. But when you open the door you see how wet and miserable it is and you hesitate, which doesn't feel too good because, really, all we are talking about here is *Running in the Rain. Seriously… how hard can it be?*

# CHAPTER 1

# Stay in Your Zone

*The Energy of the Mind is the Essence of Life.*

**–Aristotle**

It was almost completely dark now, except for the streetlights that seem to be much more spread out when you are on your feet than when you are in your car, but it can be fun to run in the dark as you often get the sense you are going faster.

The sound of my feet beating into the hard pavement reinforced the steady pace of the progress I was making towards my goal of completing my first Ironman triathlon. I turned right onto Highway 60 heading east out of Huntsville – a small town on the edge of the Ontario wilderness – and the fresh northern air filled my lungs. I glanced at my Garmin watch: I was 6 miles from the finish line, with about 134 miles behind me now. My legs were weary, my sensitive parts were suffering the effects of a little too much athletic friction and I was hungry. I was done with gels and energy snacks. I was on the verge of completion.

One hour to go and I would be done. I had saved a special musical treat for this very corner – John Williams's stirring composition, "Summon the Heroes," which he had composed for the 1996 Atlanta Olympics. It was one of my favourite inspirational pieces of music and I had worked hard to keep it from my mind up to this point. No iPods or phones were allowed for this race, but the music reverberated through my head causing me to accelerate and start passing the runners who had been passing me for the last half hour or so.

About 50 minutes later I could not only see the lights of the finish chute laid out at Deerhurst Resort, but I could hear the announcer calling out his immortal words of triumphant encouragement as triathletes crossed the finish line in jubilation. I beat my way up the final hill, my legs pumping and my lungs bursting, and I tore around the last bend to charge down the last few yards of the course and meet the roaring crowd. It was a moment I had been waiting a year to experience *"Paul Weston – YOU ARE AN IRONMAN."* I crossed the finish line in a blaze of flashes from the cameras held by numerous photographers and revelled in some serious back-slapping and calls of congratulations. It was one of the best and most euphoric events of my life.

I was gathered up by a volunteer who ensured I felt okay and asked if I needed any medical assistance but thankfully all was well, despite the fact I had spent the last 13 hours and 50 minutes completing a 2.5-mile swim, a 112-mile bike course, and a full 26-mile marathon. I grabbed a bottle of water and my medal and picked up the standard-issue finisher's swag, which consisted of a hat and a t-shirt. Then I headed out of the athlete's zone to exchange some rather sweaty hugs with my wife and dash off a quick video for my parents. I stretched my legs and we headed off to our accommodation for the night, where I got cleaned up and enjoyed a late supper and a couple of beers.

Ready for Sleep?

And so, after completing my first Ironman Triathlon, I was ready for bed and a good night's sleep – who wouldn't be, right?

Wrong.

I lay down on our Airbnb bed expecting to float nicely off, but I was wired, and sleep enthusiastically eluded me.

The reason? Endorphins, my own private narcotic. Endorphins are neurotransmitters, chemicals that pass signals from one neuron to the next. Neurotransmitters play a key role in the function of the central nervous system and can either prompt or suppress the further signaling of nearby neurons.

In the early 1970s, researchers studying how the brain is affected by opiates such as heroin or morphine found that they interact with specialized receptors in cells that are primarily massed in the brain and spinal cord. When opiates enter these receptors, they hinder or block the cell's transmission of pain signals. But the scientists studying this phenomenon wondered why these specialized receptors existed in the first place The most plausible answer was that opioid receptors exist due to the presence of an opiate-like substance produced naturally in the body – and levels of that substance had been building and growing inside me for the previous 14 hours.

As I lay there, you could almost hear those endorphins pinging around the room.

I tossed, I turned and of course, I started to rerun in my mind whole chunks of the day, with the bonus of "Summon the Heroes" playing repeatedly in my head.

Endorphins are produced as a response to certain stimuli, especially stress, fear, or pain. They originate in various parts of your body – like your pituitary gland, your spinal cord, and other parts of your brain and nervous system – and, as mentioned earlier, they interact mainly with receptors in cells found in regions of the brain responsible for blocking pain and controlling emotion. Until recently, much of what we've learned about endorphins has been gained from monitoring them in the human bloodstream and the brains of rats. It wasn't possible to measure endorphin levels in the human brain without harming the subject, so the role of endorphins in the phenomenon of the "runner's high" and other periods of euphoria or mood change were still being hotly debated at the time. However, there was no debate here – the damned things weren't going to let me sleep no matter how hard I tried.

I had experienced this before, of course. Sports had played a key part in my life from an early age, mostly through rugby, cricket and golf, and although I had won a few trophies here and there, and had played on some pretty good teams in some very competitive leagues, I had forgotten the effects of the rush that hits you after experiencing a high-quality victory.

And I didn't have to win to be an endorphin victim. I immigrated to Canada in 2005 at the age of 42 and thought I would try my hand at ice hockey, joining a house league that played on Monday evenings.

Because of the popularity of the game, and the limited ice time available, there were some weeks when our games would start at 11:00 p.m., which meant I would get to bed around 1:00 a.m. after an hour of extremely high-intensity sport. Whether we won or lost – and we usually lost – I would hardly get a minute's sleep. And so, over the last few years, I have started to consider how the Mental Energy generated by physical activity can be harnessed in a fashion that allows for improved functionality and productivity, all in a general attempt to see how I could get more stuff done.

## Don't *Find* time – *Schedule* it

As a business owner and an endurance athlete, I am often asked how I manage my time in order to complete my professional responsibilities as well as get the training under my belt to allow me to compete in Ironman Triathlons and other events.

And although I benefit from the genetics of my parents – both of whom are extremely well-organized – and the advantage of a disciplined attitude developed during a 26-year military career, I can't *manage time*, I can only manage the attention I place on specific tasks and, in particular, where I place my energy and personal resources. The questions I ask myself are:

- How important is this task to me?
- What impact will this specific task have on my day, week, month, year or career?
- Who is dependent upon my completion of the task?

All of these components can define where I decide to allocate my energy resources and, in many cases, they will define success through the routines and systems I put in place – I will discuss these in more detail later. In essence, though, when someone asks me how I find time to train, I answer that I don't *find* time to train. I *schedule* it.

## Our Three Energy Zones

I have a theory. As I mentioned in the introduction to this book, I believe we divide the actions we take in every minute of our lives into three categories:

## Professional, Personal and Social

Our **Professional Energy Zone** is where we execute the tasks for which we are professionally responsible and accountable. In this zone we do our job, complete our strategic objectives, meet our targets, and communicate with our colleagues, managers, subordinates and internal and external customers. We lead and manage our teams, sell our products, undertake personal development tasks relating to our career, attend conferences, engage in meetings and complete all the other activities that help us earn a buck and keep a roof over our heads.

Our **Personal Energy Zone** is the place in which we do all the "me" stuff.

Into this category fall our weekly yoga class, our personal fitness regime or daily walk, our meditation or spiritual pursuits in their many forms, the reading of books, sleeping and even driving to work. In other words, anything that results in being alone doing an activity that involves only you – and which preferably benefits you – falls into your Personal Energy Zone.

As a triathlete, I love the individuality of the sport and although race day can involve diving into a lake with thousands of other competitors, once I am moving the race is really just about me and my own personal effort.

Our **Social Energy Zone**, by contrast, is a place where we do pretty much everything else as it will generally involve other people. Family mealtimes, meeting friends for dinner, playing golf with the usual gang, team sports, barbecues, church or group worship activities, community events such as volunteering, arts or musical endeavours like singing in a choir, playing in an orchestra and performing in a play – these are all typical examples of what we do in our Social Energy Zone.

## Zone Dilution

By now you may be thinking about your own Energy Zones and considering how to define each activity you perform and where they all fit.

I've given something of a general view above to get things started and although you can – if you try hard enough – be very specific about what zone you find yourself in, it really shouldn't be too difficult to determine at any one point in time. For example, if I am at work then surely I am in my Professional Zone, right? Yes, as long as everything you are doing is what you have been hired to do, or is having a direct impact on your business. But what happens if you are updating your CRM, reading an email from a customer, or watching a webinar about a new product you are about to launch, and your phone buzzes and you see a text from your partner?

Is it part of your job to answer that text? Well, unless you both work for the same company, or your partner is a supplier or customer, then it probably isn't your paid job to answer that text, and so consequently, by opening said text, you have just diluted your Professional Zone with your Social Zone.

And what happens if you are sitting on your deck on a beautiful summer evening with the house and garden to yourself, reading a fascinating book that you are truly enjoying about a topic about which you are passionate, and your phone buzzes again?

You look down and it is an email from your manager.

You are done with work and you are at home alone in a wonderful place with a great book. In other words, you are deeply into your Personal Energy Zone when that email arrives, and the minute your eyes are taken from the written text of the book to that email alert, you are diluting your Personal Zone with your Professional Zone.

What if you are out with your family to celebrate your son's birthday at his favourite local steak house, and you are all sitting around a table looking at the menu when your phone buzzes with a text alert that the San Francisco Giants, a team for whom no one else in your family cares, is leading 1 – 0 after the First Inning?

If you are the only family member who cares about the Giants, then any attention you pay to incoming text score updates during that family celebration is diluting your Social Zone with your Personal Zone.

Now, I am not suggesting for one minute that you should *never* answer a text from your partner while you are at work, that you should *never* check a work email of an evening, or you should *never* check the baseball score while you are out with your family, but unless you develop some form of system to manage when you *do* decide to leave your Zone – even if it is just for a few seconds – then you are allowing yourself to be taken out through actions you are not controlling, which is where it can start going south.

## Where It All Starts To Go Wrong

All of the above examples are typical, and we can all be guilty of most of them.

Many companies require everyone to put their phones in a pile at the beginning of meetings to stop the dilution of Professional Zones with Personal and Social.

Some golf courses ban mobile phones – in fact, I used to play at a club where using your phone on the course would cost you a two-stroke penalty. And many families insist that phones are not allowed at the dinner table. But while these rules are made with the best intentions in mind, are they carried over to someone's own individual Professional,

Personal, or Social Zones? Because if not, then their zones will become diluted to the detriment of efficiency, functionality, and productivity, to the detriment of the benefits of personal objectives and to the detriment of social activities, on which we all depend.

Zone Recognition is a key aspect of this topic and will be explored in more detail later, but one of the great benefits of understanding which zone you are engaged in is the productivity that may then be achieved as a result.

When we consider productivity, we would typically associate it with our Professional Zone, but it can just as easily be applied to our Personal and Social Zones.

If I am training for a long endurance event, there are rarely any shortcuts I can adopt in order to be fully prepared for race day. I have to put in long hours in the pool, on the bike, and running on the roads and trails. This is productivity in my Personal Zone, as is getting through that book while sitting on my deck or completing three yoga classes each week.

Each of these are examples of Personal Zone productivity.

As a member of a community orchestra, I would expect to be engaged in rehearsals each week and several concerts each season – again, these are simply examples of Social Zone productivity, and this isn't just about meeting my company's strategic objectives, it is about producing the energy in my Personal and Social Zones in order to lead a fulfilling and rewarding lifestyle.

But where does it start to go wrong?

You don't have to be a passionate sports fan to have heard of some global sporting champion being *"in the zone."* This refers to them having the ability to close out any other thought and focus on the task at hand, to put a barrier around them that excludes any distractions that could deter them from peak performance.

Of course, pretty much every professional sportsperson today will have some form of psychological support expert in their camp, as the world of sports psychology has developed exponentially over the last few decades; thankfully it is not just about being *"in the zone"* that matters, but what format that zone may take – are you fully focused, distracted or just not really *present?*

I can remember playing on a rugby team whose coach was about as passionate and determined as ever a coach could be. Training meant we were often pushed to our breaking point; commitment to the cause was one dimensional – you were either all in or all out – and our match days were great if we won, as we celebrated as hard as we trained, but they were not much fun if we lost.

And, of course, victories were accompanied by the onset of an endorphin overload and not a lot of sleep.

The problem was that for around 30 minutes before kickoff, our inimitable coach would build us up to the point where we were so overloaded with adrenalin that if it were physically possible, most of us would have literally walked through the locker room wall to get on to the pitch. Did this make us play better? Not really. Some team members would be out of control and for the first 20 minutes we would give away so many penalties that we would be chasing a losing cause for the rest of the game.

I was in the military at the time and eventually moved cities to join another team whose coach knew the importance of individual drive. He would study each player in order to understand what made them tick. On match days he would give some players a good push to get their "game faces" on; he would leave others alone to focus on their own pre-game process. Great performance psychologists recognize the individual in all their subjects, and we will explore the topic of focus, and being "in the zone," in a later chapter.

## The Implications of Zone Dilution

For most of us, Zone Dilution has major implications – we don't want to get knocked out of the Zone in which we are trying to remain, in which we are trying to be productive, in which others are dependent on us or in which we badly want to achieve something. Why not? Simple: if we don't produce or succeed, the implication this "failure" has on our mindset can be significant.

Had I not completed my first Ironman Triathlon I would have been extremely disappointed. I knew there was always the chance of a race-ending crash or a mechanical breakdown on the bike, or an injury in the swim or on the run, but many of those outcomes can be alleviated with efficient and well-planned preparation. If I had simply not completed the distance through insufficient training, however, or by not following a disciplined nutrition plan or by failing to adhere to a schedule designed to prepare me to get from start to finish within the allotted time frame, it almost certainly would have been because I did not spend enough time in my Personal Energy Zone in order to train. Or perhaps it might have been the result of not using the time I did spend in that Zone wisely, or even allowing the Zone to be continually diluted by activities that belonged in other zones.

Indeed, there have been occasions when I have cut short a bike ride to return to my home office to respond efficiently to a work email that could easily have been handled later that day. Other times my phone has buzzed while I've been on a run and I've stopped to check it. I've seen a text from my wife, and I've responded, which then required several more interactions, by which time I was cold and rather than continue, I've turned around and headed home. I've also seen emails come in from clients at 6:30 a.m. as I sat parked outside the local swimming pool, ready for a two-hour swim session. I've decided I wanted to respond from my laptop, so I've cut my training by half and returned to my office an hour earlier than planned to send an email that could easily have waited a few hours, never mind just one.

Life will always throw us curve balls over which we have no control and there will be times when we simply *have* to leave whichever specific Zone we are in. But, having looked into the work and lifestyle practices of many, many, people, I can safely say that pretty much everyone I have ever come across can take more action to stay in the right zone at the right time in order to be more "productive," regardless of whether they are working on professional goals, personal desires or family responsibilities.

## Creating Gold Medal Winning Weeks

Imagine it is late Friday afternoon – say around 5:00 p.m. You are done for the day and you are done for the week. So, how do you feel?

Have you staggered over the line, desperately glad it is the end of the week – a week like no other – and felt that if, in fact, you have many more like that one, you need to seriously consider your future? You got behind on most of your tasks. Yesterday you met with a customer who was so angry and upset you feared they may have become physically violent. You were in several meetings that dragged on for so long you started to lose the will to live. Your boss distracted you so many times you didn't know what to do next and it felt like you were living in a constant nightmare of "mission creep."

OR, are you full of energy and can't wait for Monday morning to roll around again? While you feel physically tired, from a Professional Energy Zone perspective, it has been a remarkably productive week. You hit every target. You landed five new accounts and your CRM is all up to date. All those customer feedback forms have been read and documented, the strategic plan for next year is now fully drafted, all your team's performance evaluations are complete and signed, you are exceeding your sales targets and the new product launch is ahead of schedule and looking good. You even had lunch with your boss who is delighted with the progress your team is making. The future looks very bright. You have put in some intense hours, but the drive home feels good and while you are ready to kick back on the weekend, you have a certain "buzz" about your feelings. Your deck awaits along with a glass of something very rewarding as a means to round off a week during which you feel like you have won a Gold Medal.

Creating *Gold Medal Winning Weeks* are unlikely to generate enough endorphins to keep you awake on Friday nights – in fact, it is more likely that disaster weeks will generate enough worry to get in the way of a good night's sleep. But one thing those winning weeks will do is fill up your Mental Energy resources, no matter how physically drained you may be.

## Physical Drain for Marathon Gains

*It is 9:30 a.m. on Sunday, October 29, 2017, and I am about to do something really stupid.*

*I am standing in the middle of thousands of runners at the start of the Scotiabank Toronto Waterfront Marathon, which in itself is not particularly stupid, except for the fact that I have a 20–pound pack strapped to my upper body (if you are not sure of the implications of that weight, think of it as being the same as 10-two-pound bags of sugar). The natural question here, is: why?*

*Well, around 10 years earlier, I had been diagnosed with osteoarthritis in my knees, shoulders, and lower back, which, after several decades of playing rugby, plus 26 years in the military, may not be surprising. But the impact on my body was much greater than the pain and the quarterly cortisone injections in my joints: my doctors advised me to stop pretty much all forms of activity, including running and cycling, and they told me to take a cart around the golf course rather than walk.*

*This lifestyle change had a very significant effect on me: I gained some weight, which made the pain even worse. But in 2012 I thought I would give the Paleo Diet a try and removed wheat and grains from my diet, among other changes. I found the results to be really quite miraculous in that not only did the pain from my arthritis almost completely disappear but in less than two weeks I had shed more than 20 pounds of weight. It meant that I could return to more physical activity. A few months later I was offered the chance to run a 10-kilometre race in Toronto with a friend, upon completion of which I realized I was able to get back to running and, subsequently, back into some serious cycling. The lifestyle change represented a decisive moment for me and over the next few years I went on to complete several marathons, four Ironman triathlons and I ultimately qualified for Team Canada's participation in the 2019 Duathlon World Championships in Pontevedra, Spain.*

*Along the way, in early 2017, I decided to look for inspiration watching some old Royal Marines documentaries on YouTube and the experience led me to wonder* *if I had the strength and determination to do something extra, something different, something that would take me even further beyond the limits of my comfort zone. The idea of running the Toronto Marathon with a weight equivalent to the amount I had lost in 2012 cropped up and I paired it with the idea of setting a $10,000 fundraising target. I committed myself to action by starting a campaign page on The Arthritis Society website. Then I put two 10-pound dumbbells – equivalent to 4.5 kilograms – in a backpack and went for a jog. Which made me wonder what the hell I had been thinking!*

*With a bit of testing, adjusting, and experimentation, I settled for a weight vest – basically a waistcoat – and started getting my act together on the training front.*

*The fundraising went really well and about a month before the race I had exceeded my target of $10,000; I actually started the race with $11,231 in the bank, which raised a few interesting questions:*

*What if I don't finish?*

*A standard marathon is 42 kilometres (26 miles) in length. What if I break down after 30 kilometres? In order to avoid over-training and injuring myself, I had limited my long runs with the weight to 21 kilometres, so anything beyond that was a no-man's land for me.*

*Would I have to refund out of my own pocket the donations people had made?*

*And what would people think: this idiot thought he could run a marathon with 20 pounds on his back at his age – what arrogance, what stupidity, what craziness!*

*At the start of the race I lined up in the five hour finish time corral I had selected with the intention of refraining from breaking any speed records. What was interesting for me, was that I felt physically fully charged. I had put the hard miles in with the weight, I had adhered to a strong nutrition plan and I had laid off the snacks and garbage food for several months. About four weeks prior to the event I had followed recommended best practices and executed a "peak training week," where I pushed myself to the limit, then tapered my activity down with a few weeks of very low activity leading up to race day. The upshot was that I felt energized, rested and ready to go physically, at least.*

*Mentally, I was a bit of a mess.*

*I had had a decent night's sleep, but when I picked up the weight in my hotel room the morning of the race, a fear of failure swept over me. My Mental Energy Pack was very depleted.*

~

*I had recruited some friends to run alongside me when I attempted the Load Carry Marathon. One was attempting his first marathon[1] and the other two were experienced runners and multiple Ironman finishers[2]. Any support team is important, but I was also concerned that they might become frustrated with the slow pace we would be running, which was an added worry on my mind.*

*The race started and we set off at a reasonable pace. In fact, probably a little too fast, because we were through the 10-kilometre mark in just under an hour. And at this point, there was a major shift in the status of my Physical and Mental Energy.*

*The quarter distance point was a significant mark. It told me we were on target for a time of around five hours – which I considered quite reasonable considering the load I was carrying. A body system check revealed my back was starting to ache a little and the backpack's shoulder straps were rubbing slightly, but my legs were doing okay and felt strong. Most importantly, my Mental Energy status – my Mental Battery Pack – was starting to charge up. I had checked off a quarter of the distance and I felt okay, so maybe I could keep this going.*

*The second most emotional point in the Toronto Waterfront Marathon is the approach to the halfway mark. You run along Lakeshore Boulevard and two large inflatable mileage markers appear in the distance at the bottom of Bay Street. There are volunteers in the centre of the road. They tell runners who are doing the Half Marathon to stay to the left, and those doing the Full Marathon to keep right. The inflatables are marked "Half" and "Full" to ensure runners take the correct course.*

*I had convinced Ahmad to sign up for the full marathon by asking how he would feel turning left as the rest of us kept right and continued on our way, abandoning*

---

[1] Ahmad Zbib, Executive Director, Ontario Division, The Arthritis Society
[2] Andrea Sorensen and Vilija Hakala.

*him and his lack of ambition. He had fallen for it, and he now pointed to the signage with a grin as we passed beneath it and headed south, then east.*

*The halfway point in any endurance event is a key landmark and this gave me the chance for another systems check. My back was aching a little more and my shoulders were about the same, but my legs were starting to feel the strain now. As 21-kilometres was the furthest I had run in training, I was now heading into new territory, but, most notably, a smile was starting to build in my subconscious as I was really beginning to feel that I might actually be able to do this thing.*

*In other words, my Mental Energy status – my Mental Battery Pack – was now above 50% charged even though my Physical Energy was waning.*

*The most emotionally demanding part of the Toronto Waterfront Marathon route arises during the 10-kilometres after the halfway mark that leads away from the finish line you have quite recently nearly passed. Fortunately, at around the 30-kilometre point, you take a 180-degree left turn and head back towards the city again, and this has a significantly positive impact on your psyche. It's not technically all downhill from here (it's actually a very flat course), but at this point, you are at least heading in the right direction and are well on your way to completing the race. For me, that turn was inspiring. There were large crowds gathered alongside the course at this point, including several friends who had come out to cheer me on knowing I would probably need some moral support to get through the last quarter of the race.*

*By now my back was starting to seize up a bit, my shoulders were rubbing quite significantly and there were clearly some blisters just above my hips from the weight bouncing up and down. My legs were not really shaking, but they were certainly feeling more wooden with each step. But my watch said there were only 10-kilometres left in the marathon and it was time to start humming "Summon the Heroes" again. My Mental Energy source was really pumped now.*

*The crowds watching the last few kilometres of the marathon were loud, and I was spurred on by their enthusiasm. Although my legs were almost done, the shouts and screams echoed around the outer walls of the downtown financial district like some angelic choir amid an epic oratorio. Small handbells rattled amongst the masses as our small team approached the final bend and it felt as though we were on the slopes of an alpine World Cup downhill ski race. The finish line was upon us almost immediately and we grabbed hands together and raised them in celebration as we crossed the line, united in our victorious assault on the race, precisely 4:59:57 after we started. This was to be the slowest marathon of my life, but it was also the toughest.*

*With medals placed over our heads, bottles of water in our hands, and foil blankets around our shoulders, we headed to the post-race meeting point to rejoin our friends and family members, the battle won, the money earned and my task accomplished. The journey home was agony, marked by constant leg cramps, but I had completed what I had set out to accomplish six months previously: run a marathon carrying a 20-pound weight and raise $10,000 for The Arthritis Society. My Physical Energy Source was completely drained, but inside, my Mental Battery Pack was buzzing with charge – and another endorphin-filled sleepless night was ahead of me.*

## Physical Drain for Mental Gain at Work

How does the idea of physical drain for mental gain equate to your workweek?

Let's say you have had a good weekend – maybe you enjoyed a barbecue and a few drinks with friends, or headed to the beach with the family, played some golf, got the garden tidied up, started or finished that Netflix series – or binge-watched the whole thing – and you are rested and energized for the new week.

Now it's Monday morning and you have just arrived at the office, switched on your PC, made a coffee, checked in with some of your colleagues, logged in, opened your inbox, and started to make a To-Do list for the day and week ahead. (I will be showing you later how to live a life without To-Do lists!)

The first activities that come to mind are probably the tasks you didn't complete last week, so you are playing catch–up from the start. You look at some looming project deadlines. You have another pile of meetings to attend this week, a challenging customer coming to see you on Wednesday, you have a disciplinary matter to tend to with a member of your team, your HR manager is making noises about getting the performance evaluations completed on time and your CEO has asked you to read several reports and make recommendations to her by Thursday.

The week is not looking good and although you feel physically ready to get going, your Mental Energy Pack is now not so strong. In fact, it feels like you are standing at the start of a marathon with a 20 pound weight vest strapped to you.

We rely on the team around us and others are, of course, reliant upon us for our productivity. That daunting week ahead can impose additional pressure when we realize we have to support others in their work, and others are waiting for us to complete our projects to the required standard and on time.

It is Tuesday lunchtime in the office, and you do your own Professional Zone system check. You have completed a significant number of the tasks that were laid in front of you on Monday morning. The performance evaluations are well underway, and your team member has accepted responsibility for their misdemeanor and is taking your advice. They actually thanked you for your care and attention. You still have a very busy week ahead, with several new projects coming your way, but the deadlines that were looming on Monday are now looking much more reasonable. You decide to step out of the office for lunch with an old friend you haven't seen for a few years and, as you walk, you realize the week is actually going pretty well. Your Mental Energy status – your Mental Battery Pack – is starting to charge up a bit.

Although Tuesday lunchtime in the office may have felt good, the rest of that day also went well and on Wednesday morning you completed the reports for your boss a day early, handled the nightmare customer really well – to the point where they seemed very satisfied with your proposal and renewed their contract – and although there were a few fastballs thrown your way, you kept things moving and your team responded with lots of enthusiasm.

It is halfway through a week that has been very busy, but you are feeling great about how you are able to function and how productive you are being. Your Mental Energy status – your Mental Battery Pack – which was pretty low on Monday morning, is now above 50% charged, even though you are Physically starting to feel tired, considering the amount of work you are getting done.

It is Thursday evening, and you do a quick system check. Your lists are well under control, your CEO replied to say the reports you wrote are all looking good, you have all your performance evaluations complete, signed off, and sent to HR and while a few more fastballs came your way, you handled them well without creating too much extra work.

There is only one day left in the week and you have a little capacity to spend some time with your team and fully connect before the weekend. You feel good – it's been a great week and Friday should be a very pleasant day, something to look forward to and a great way to end the week. You close the office and head for home feeling strong.

Arriving in the office on a Friday when you have enjoyed a very productive week is rather a nice feeling. The dress code is relaxed, the team is looking forward to the weekend and the office sun is shining. You have time to clean up a few loose ends from Thursday, huddle up with your team to plan your POETS[3] day, start some of the long-term

---

[3] Push Off Early Tomorrow's Saturday – this is a system that provides a great incentive to increase productivity on a Friday in order to finish the work week a few hours early.

strategic planning you've had sitting on the horizon for a few weeks now and develop a clear focus for the following week. You are quite tired as you have managed to complete a lot of work this week, but although your Physical Energy Source is pretty drained and ready for the weekend, you manage to work all day humming with the warm feeling of a job well done.

$$\sim$$

The principle of *Physical Drain 4 Mental Gain* involves the transfer of energy from the physical realm to the mental realm. As noted earlier, heavy physical activity is likely to create endorphins, the fitness drug we all love, which feed the brain to the point where sleep can be very difficult. It is unlikely the positive energy generated from a successful week's work will deny anyone sleep, but the Friday Night feel-good factor generated from a good week is akin to the Finish Line feel-good factor so many athletes experience after completing endurance events.

The key to reaching these levels of high productivity, however, is the ability to first recognize the Energy Zones in which we spend different aspects of our lives, and then to develop the capacity to remain within them in order to complete the relevant tasks set out for us. The final challenge is to be functional while in each Zone so that when we leave one, we know we have been successful and efficient, and we have focused our energy in a way that allows us to master our time.

The remainder of this book is designed to help you get in the right zone, harness your energy and create *Gold Medal Winning Weeks*.

Rather like *Running in the Rain*, we may not like the thought of it, it doesn't always look fun, but once we get our shoes on and get out there, it's not so bad... and when it's over, we can feel pretty good about what we just did.

# CHAPTER 2

# Goals Really Stink

*If you are too busy to build good systems, then you will always be too busy.*

**–Brian Logue**

*I*f *Running in the Rain* sounds so unappealing, and most people wouldn't do it, then why should anyone bother? There is a number of reasons I could give to answer this question and you may think I run in the rain because I have a goal. But the trouble with that is… goals stink.

I'm sorry, but if you came here to be inspired to set and achieve some amazing and life-changing goals, you wasted your money, because… goals stink.

You are standing on the fourth tee with a long par five in front of you. There is water down the left, some heavy rough down the right and a fairly narrow tee down the middle. In order to get on the green in no more than three shots, you have to put your drive on the short grass.

Your goal is pretty simple: put the ball on the fairway.

You drive, and your old friend the *pull* visits you, the ball sails left and makes a tidy splash in Lake Desperation.

Goals stink.

◠

It's Friday evening and you are having dinner with your husband. You discuss what the weekend should look like and you tell him you plan to get the backyard cleaned up, plant some new shrubs and prune the rose bushes. Your goal is simple: get the back yard looking good.

On Saturday you realize you need to get groceries, so you head out late morning to join with the metropolis of people in the same boat. It takes hours to get done and get home. Once home you stow the groceries away and answer a call from your sister (you had forgotten she was scheduled to call) and then spend an hour chatting about teenage daughters. Later, you escape to see an email from a client asking for a quote on a project as soon as possible. This could be a very good opportunity, so you open up your laptop and get to work.

The quote is finished and sent, but while you are there, you check some more emails (just to keep on top of things), which takes up another hour, after which you realize it is probably time for a glass of wine and the yard can wait for Sunday.

On Sunday it rains all day, and the yard will have to wait another week.

Goals stink.

◠

Joe and his wife Pat were driving home from her brother's house after a reasonably pleasant weekend during which Pat's brother, Bill, had completed his first Tough Mudder.[4] Bill was the toast of the family for completing such a challenging event and all the talk on Saturday evening

---

[4] A Tough Mudder is an endurance event where competitors run through mud and carry heavy weights over obstacles, among other challenges.

around the barbecue was how much training and effort he had put in, how his body had changed and how fit he was looking. Joe used to play running back on his college football team and although he had come close (in his mind) to making it into the big leagues, alas it had never happened. Once he graduated from college he hung his football boots up and other than the odd gentle trail ride on his mountain bike with his wife, he had lived a sedentary life for more than 10 years.

Joe now weighed around 230 pounds, about 60 pounds more than he had weighed when he had played football. Bill had also been overweight, but the last few months had seen him make some significant improvements in his general health and fitness.

Joe and Pat's journey home took around three hours and as they pulled into their driveway, Joe turned to his wife and said, "I'm going to do it."

"What?" she asked.

"A Tough Mudder," Joe responded.

"Yeah right," Pat said, "It'll kill you."

"Thanks – but I am," Joe said, "Even if it kills me, I am going to do it."

And so started a six-month period leading towards what was to be one of the toughest days of Joe's life. He searched for a trainer, who put him in touch with a nutritionist, who connected him with a Registered Massage Therapist (RMT), who recommended a Chiropractor, who advised he also do some yoga. It was quite the team, and Pat soon started to realize her husband was serious; she admired him for the positive changes he was making.

Joe's trainer recommended some build-up races and while he was never going to break any records, all the work he was putting in was starting to pay off: he managed to finish every race while dropping several clothes sizes in the process.

## Race Day

And then, it was race day. Pat's family made an effort to reciprocate and travelled across the country to cheer Joe on. Bill was there, still looking good and now heavily into training for his next event: a *Tougher* Mudder (there's always one who has to take things a step further); he was equally impressed with Joe's determination.

Joe, now weighing in at 170 pounds, felt good as he arrived at the start. His plan for the day was simple: to complete the Tough Mudder course within the allocated time frame.

He attacked the race from the start, made good progress, slowed a little towards the end, but finished with a huge and dirty smile. The family celebrated that evening and Joe enjoyed being the centre of attention, but his thoughts were now turning to the foods he had been missing for most of the previous few months. By the following day, he was back amongst the hamburgers, doughnuts, cakes and beer.

Why not? He had achieved what he thought was his goal; he didn't need his trainer any longer, the RMT was history, the chiropractor ridiculously expensive and he always felt out of place at yoga. Within a week he had put on 10 pounds, within two weeks, 30 pounds, and two months after completing the race, he was back at his original weight – and felt pretty bad about that.

Goals stink.

## "Our VP of Sales is an idiot."

I heard this from the sales manager of a software company in Toronto at the end of a workshop I was facilitating a few years ago. I knew her VP, although not too well, so I asked the sales manager what was going on.

"Every year he gives us these ridiculous sales targets that we *never* hit, in fact, they have been increasing every year despite the fact we haven't got within 30% of one for over four years!" she responded.

"He says the market determines the target, but if we never get close, what's the point?"

I asked her how that made the team feel and she replied that it made them feel pretty despondent, disengaged and demotivated. Despite this, they kept plugging away. But their real target was simply focused on minimizing the size of their failure, to keep the gap between their target and their results as small as possible. This is a bit like telling a soccer team that they are bound to lose, but they should try really hard not to lose by too much, if possible.

Goals stink.

Many young people growing up want to be professional sportspeople. They imagine the glory of competing at the highest level, of being selected by their favourite team, and of one day entering some theatre of dreams in the final of a major competition. Just imagine being on one of those teams and about to play in that final game. You are in the tunnel of the stadium about to walk out onto the hallowed turf, like a Roman Centurion ready to do battle to the death. (Well, maybe not quite that far, but it's a big game, anyway.)

The stadium tunnel is a heaving mass of anxiety, nerves, sweat and noise. You are trying to focus on your game and get *in your zone*, but standing alongside you is the competition, looking equally anxious, nervous, and sweaty. You try not to look at them, and they try not to look at you – but you know they are there. The mind games have begun. And, although you want to play your own game, do your own thing, and be part of your own team, there is one underlying concern within the atmosphere of expectation: your goal.

You see, you and the other team have many differences: your personnel, your coach, your supporters and more. But you also have many areas in common, the most serious of which is your *goal*. You *both* want to win the game and the championship and, of course… there is only one winner. And a couple of hours later when it is all over, one team has won. And you? Well, your team lost.

Goals stink.

## And What About SMART Goals?

You get my message?

Let's press pause and have a look at goals now. I know you can argue that we all need them, otherwise we would never get out of bed, would we? (Although I'm sure many people don't need a goal to get them up in the morning.) If we don't know what we are aiming for, how do we know if we are working *well?* The truth is, the whole goal-setting process can be really challenging.

For many years, businesses have subscribed to the SMART Goal methodology (if you have been living in a cave for the last 30 years, this stands for: Specific, Measurable, Attainable, Relevant and Time-Based). And while this principle has proved extremely useful for those who subscribe to it, there are some key components that are required to make it work. For example, everyone has to be on the same page. While a team leader may have a very clear idea of what the goal is, unless they use an effective communication tool to pass this along to their team, there will likely be a number of variables affecting outcomes.

One of the biggest mistakes people make when it comes to communication is the false belief the message has been absorbed and confirmed, so no matter how specific your goal is, if there is the slightest hint of ambiguity, then good luck with that. A SMART goal has to be shared so that it is clear and obvious, not only to those who are responsible for its execution, but to those who may be indirectly influenced by it, and who are indirectly involved in its completion.

When President John F. Kennedy was involved in planning meetings with NASA in 1962, he laid out his vision for sending a man to the moon. He made it abundantly clear that there was one very simple goal: to put a man on the moon and return him safely to Earth by the end of the decade. Everything involved in that operation was focused and targeted on one basic objective. Specific? Absolutely, but President Kennedy also ensured the goal was common knowledge, which meant failure was also going to be recognized on a global level, which heightened expectation and accountability.

Schedules are, of course, another critical determinant of a successful SMART goal process. Too many teams create goals with great intent to succeed, but without a schedule to support and address progress, they will often slip off the radar and disappear into the category entitled "We Never Got Around to That." For many teams, the failure to complete a task is often related to how they implement their strategies through specific schedules. Most of these schedules see teams walk forward to the objective, whereas something called a work-back schedule – which we'll address later – can be a wonderful tool to enable fulfillment.

What's more, some organizations are guilty of "stretch-goals:" as the team comes within sight of what had originally been considered a challenging target, the goal is reassessed and the bar is placed higher, resulting in a vacuum of enthusiasm amongst stakeholders. Remember my story about the sales manager? Her VP never lowered the target mid-year, so while the goals were never stretched, they were never attainable in the first place, either. And the VP had no intention of easing them down a little.

Every organization is different, and this is especially evident in the way goals are handled, especially at the review and assessment stages once projects are completed.

During my military career, I learned the importance of thorough and in-depth strategic planning that would prepare us for any eventuality. When presenting a plan, we were required to answer a constant barrage of *"what if?"* questions, although in reality, I believe the saying that "no plan survives first contact" is as appropriate now as it was when it was first uttered: as soon as you meet the enemy, *everything* changes, no matter how well prepared you are. Attendance at pre-operational briefings was mandatory, but while that was, of course, important, it was even more important to attend the post-operational debriefs, as reviewing the *lessons learned* was the only way to ensure – as much as possible – that mistakes were never repeated.

When it comes to goals in business, I rarely see organizations thoroughly review and assess how they performed with regard to the goals that were set, in order to reset and proceed. And, without considering the points outlined here, even SMART goals can stink.

But the biggest and stinkiest part of goals is the impact they can have on us when we fail to achieve them.

That weight-loss goal you spectacularly failed to reach? Diets are awful things. The basement renovation you were going to complete before the winter set in? Still not done. The new job you were going to find? Still plugging away at the same old desk.

By now you are probably a bit fed up with my negativity regarding goals, correct? So, let me try to be positive. Goals are great when you meet them. Happy now? *But* (you knew that was coming), they are short term. Achieving a goal only delivers short-term happiness.

You want to run a marathon? Six months later you do it, well done. Now what?

You want to lose weight? Six months later you look and feel great. Now what?

You want a new job? You walk into your new office six months later. Now what?

You hit your annual sales target? Wonderful. Guess what? Next year will be even tougher.

You want to get your garden looking great? Done – now you have to maintain it every week, cut the grass, do the weeding and take out the dead plants.

Yes, we all need goals, but what is their *true* purpose? Well, hold that thought for a moment, and let's take a look at other aspects of success that are perhaps even more fundamental to the levels of satisfaction we can achieve in our Professional, Personal or Social Zones.

## The Value of Routines

I really like a good routine.

Call me boring. Call me pedantic. Call me a stick in the mud.

I don't care.

Routines make me feel warm. They relax me. They reassure me. They help me sleep. They help me perform well. They make me a better person to live with.

When I am training, I record every activity into a log. It's pretty easy these days, as a decent watch means you just have to "stop and save" and it uploads to an app that measures everything. But to effectively assess my progress, I like to train on the same routes all the time so I can truly gauge my performance. That's not to say I do the exact same distance on the exact same road or trail every single day. No, I have several options, but I can tell by looking at the time when I pass a certain tree or reach the top of a certain hill, how I am getting along. That routine ensures I am following a pattern that will result in success. It is interesting, as well, because sometimes my legs feel like lead but my times are good, and other times I feel great, but I am going pretty slowly.

I was brought up with routines. From getting out of bed to falling asleep, my life was generally one long routine. It provided me with a structure that served me particularly well when I joined the military because that is one routine-based environment! The routine of training in the military is to make sure you react in an automatic way. Now, to some people that may sound negative and monotonous, but in reality, if things get nasty – and they can get VERY nasty – the training takes over to the point where you react automatically.

If you pick a profession and study someone who has the highest performance levels in that field, I'll bet there is evidence of a routine that contributed to their success.

Concert pianist? How many hours do they spend practicing the same piece over and over?

Public speaker? How many hours do they spend preparing and rehearsing the same speech?

Fortune 500 CEO? How many years did it take them to develop best – practice business routines that they know will work?

Surgeon? How many years of repeating the same procedure did it take in order for them to become expert enough to save or drastically improve someone's life?

Now, I'm not suggesting that those mentioned above never change what they do, but it is their routines that lead them to realise *what* and *how* they need to change in order to improve. And it is their ability to maintain a routine that makes them so successful.

## From Good to Great in Rugby

Several years ago, after I had finished my competitive rugby playing days, I qualified as a coach. While I was going through the Rugby Football Union's program, I had the opportunity to meet and talk with some international players and coaches to discuss techniques and best practices. I had the opportunity to ask a question about something I had been interested in for many years: What makes a great player different from a good player? One of the answers was very interesting: I was told that great players can deal with the routine and, to some extent, the boredom, of a repetitive training schedule, whereas a simply good player lacks the enthusiasm required for consistent development and can easily lose focus.

From that, I realized the importance of routines and the application required to improve performance. And not only did the routine of consistent practice make people good players, but the routine of consistent practice also provided a vehicle that made them *better* players.

If you want to improve the way you do something, you could make a one-off significant change in your life. That might work, but I would suggest if you really wanted to make an improvement, then you probably want to introduce a change incrementally, bit by bit, one piece at a time.

Let's say you have always wanted to run a marathon. That seems like a great goal to set yourself. So, you find a race that is around six months away, you enter so you have made the commitment and you plan your training. Considering you may not have done any physical activity since you were at school, you are probably not going to go out and start your training with a 10-mile run. Your first time on the road may even just be a 10-minute walk, which you extend to 15 minutes on the second day, and so on, until you start jogging, and then start increasing the distance.

But you need to train daily at the beginning (the rest days come later), so you have created a routine that will enable you to build your fitness and stamina and prepare you for your goal.

Hold on a minute. Didn't I say that goals stink?

Of course, they do, especially this one, because if you don't complete the marathon for whatever reason, you will agree that the challenge stank; if you do complete it, then, as discussed above, it may become a short-term fix – a quick high – and then you go back to where you were six months ago: probably serious couch potato material.

So how does a routine benefit you?

Your training schedule would have meant you were being active pretty much every day. Assuming you weren't cheating on yourself, you will start to feel pretty good. You will have more Physical and Mental Energy – here come those pesky endorphins again – and you will probably lose some weight and start looking good, too; your family and friends will start seeing you in a different light.

Why would you throw all that away just because you ran 26 miles with a few thousand people? You have made running part of your life, are you going to quit on it now? Maybe you will run the marathon again next year. Maybe you can beat your time. Another race at another venue? Bring it on!

What has now happened? Running is now part of your *routine*. Running is now part of your *lifestyle*.

I really like a good routine.

I really like a good *lifestyle*.

Who wouldn't?

## Winners, Losers and Systems

I love systems.

Let's think back to my dislike of goals. What do the winners and losers who compete against each other have in common? Each team has the same number of players. The same referee. They play on the same field of play and for the same length of the game.

But they both had the same goal (remember?).

If they both had the same goal, what's the difference that results in one winner and one loser? Well, one probably has a superior *system*. In professional sport, this could relate to how a team develops young players or teaches them best practices for nutrition. It might relate to their coaching process, how they prepare for games by assessing the strengths and weaknesses of the opposition, the game plan or the strategy – all this is part of their system.

Military personnel are experts at systems, many of which date back several centuries. Major corporations may have highly intricate and expensively-drafted strategic plans, but don't let them fool you, they are basically *systems*.

I have been coaching sales representatives for several years on the finer points of selling a particular leadership development program, the methodology of which has evolved over 30 years. The system has been proven to work and the top performers within the network, without exception, follow it. I can predict the success of a newcomer to the business by the way in which they accept and apply the system and those who decide they have a better way of doing it fail – again, without exception.

If I had been glued to my couch for over a decade and now decided it was time to change things up, I can be as serious as I want about running a marathon, but if I don't find a system that works for me, then it almost certainly isn't going to work.

When we plan, prepare, cook, and serve an ambitious meal to our family and friends, we don't just look at a recipe and hope for the best. We adopt a system that would likely involve listing the ingredients, assessing what we already have in the house, going grocery shopping, doing some time appreciation based on when we shall be serving the meal, preparing it and cooking it.

Do chefs have systems? They'd better!

Do top sportsmen and women have systems that help them prepare for a competition? Of course they do.

Do Fortune 500 CEOs have systems that aid in delivering acceptable returns for their shareholders? You bet they do.

If I am entering a major multisport event that takes place sometime in the future, I apply a very defined system to help me prepare so I know I will be able to complete the event, and compete against my adversaries and the clock while improving upon my previous best time.

But (I hear you ask), aren't routines and systems the same thing? And they sound a bit like goals as well, don't they? Stick with me a little while longer and let's distinguish between them all.

## The What – The Why – The How

Goals, routines, systems… you might be thinking, "Well, they're all very interesting, but what do they have to do with each other?" Okay, I haven't really presented any profound statements yet, so here goes:

A *Goal* is simply a measurement tool for assessing whether your *System* for creating a *Routine* that will enhance your life… is actually working.

These three concepts are intricately related in setting out to create fulfillment in any area of your life. The correlate to:

- *What* you are going to do
- *Why* you are doing it and
- *How* you go about it

The WHAT is your Goal – *what* you want to achieve – and it relates to ambition and desire. One of those ambitions could be to run a marathon for example, or you could have a desire to do more yoga.

Your WHY is about the *lifestyle* you want to maintain for yourself and it's the motivating force that leads you to develop *routines*. So your WHY is very directly related to the development of routines that please you. Having the ambition to run a marathon is not really just about running a marathon and stopping, it is about creating a routine that leads to a generally healthier lifestyle. And doing more Yoga is about feeling better, more relaxed, so your routine is also related to a healthier lifestyle.

The HOW is your *system* because, in order to achieve your goal and develop a lifestyle/routine, you need a *system*. Which, for running a marathon, would be lifestyle changes and a training regimen, and for Yoga, scheduling and attending classes so many times a week.

Every now and then, you assess your goal to test if your system is working. You have either completed your goal = the system works, or you haven't = the system is broken.

Easy, eh? Great.

Let's go back to cooking that magnificent meal for your friends.

- Your *goal* (the *what*) is to serve the meal.
- Your *routine* (the *why*) is to be seen as a more than competent cook and to be a kind and generous host.
- Your *system* (the *how*) is the process you follow in order to prepare and serve the meal, not once, but any time the opportunity presents itself.

Did you achieve your goal by serving a wonderful meal? If yes, then you will be recognized as a great cook and generous host – your system works. Did the meal stink? You are not seen as a good cook – therefore, your system failed.

Let's go back to Joe and his Tough Mudder.

- His *goal* (the *what*) was to complete the race.
- His *routine* (the *why*) could have been a new lifestyle, but unlike his brother-in-law Bill whose routine/lifestyle was to keep challenging himself with an even tougher race – Joe slipped back to his former lifestyle.
- His *system* (the *how*) only functioned in the short term and he ended up back at his original weight, eating the same old garbage – and having to deal with long-term failure.

The VP of Sales was obsessed with his goals each year. The *what* was easy on paper. It was clearly just an arbitrary number that no one even got close to achieving for more than four years. His desired *routine* (the *why*) was to be seen as an effective sales executive who drove his team by setting demanding targets – i.e. that was what he *wished* his professional *lifestyle* to be.

But his *system* (the *how*) was not fit for his purpose, because when you use the goal as a measurement tool, and you have failed, then that tells you your *system* is broken. And in this case, the VP's team members were becoming more and more disengaged from their work and were likely to burn out or leave for a job with a company with systems in place that allow for the successful execution of their goals.

## SMART Goals Test a System

We looked at SMART goals earlier and they are a fine example of testing a system. In fact, they are an excellent method of not only testing the system but of defining the precise point at which it has broken.

- Specific: Have we completed exactly what we set out to achieve?
- Measurable: If we failed, then by how much? This tells us how badly broken the system is.

- Attainable: Did the system get us close or were we completely out of our depth?

- Relevant: Has there been a significant mission-creep? In this case, the system has shown us we need to set goals that are more suitable to either our needs or our abilities.

- Time-Based: Was the system capable of delivering the goal but the time allocation was simply not enough, or are there other resources required before this can be attempted again?

The above are simply examples of how the *goal* might be used to test the *system* because, without a working *system*, the only *goals* that are scored are likely to be flukes.

~

You might be sitting there thinking, "This is great information, Paul, but what does this have to do with Energy Zones and productivity?" Thank you for asking! And here is the answer: Remaining productive in a specific area (Professional, Personal or Social) is a nice goal to have, whether we are at work, focusing on a *me* task at home or in a social environment with our family around the dinner table.

But this is only great insofar as the goal supports the routines (lifestyles) we wish to create, e.g. being productive at work in order to *complete projects on time*, *improving our health* by attending at least three yoga classes a week or *building a stronger social unit* by ensuring we gather for a family meal each day. And in order to create and maintain those routines, we need to create *systems* that allow them to function effectively – in each and every Zone.

~

We have considered the issue of *goals* in our lives, which is *what* we want to do. And the virtues of *routines* which are effectively our lifestyle – the *why* of what we do. And the *how* of our *systems* in executing those *goals*. *Running in the Rain* is basically part of my system. It is the *how* of my life: I will never achieve the *goals* that will allow me to enjoy my *routines* without a *system* that enables me to overcome seemingly unpleasant experiences, like wet feet and rain in my face.

So, how do we create effective *systems* that help us achieve our *goals*, even when we are *Running in the Rain*?

First, we need something on which to *focus* – so read on!

# CHAPTER 3

# I Can See Clearly Now

*There is time enough for everything in the course of the day if you do but one thing at once; but there is not time enough in the year if you will do two things at a time.*

**— Lord Chesterfield**

*Running in the Rain* makes me feel like "I" am in control of my life. Not the weather, not someone who is telling me it is too wet to run, not addictions like social media and the internet... I don't want to exist for those people and those bad habits; I want to *live*.

In 2003 I made the life-changing decision to have laser eye surgery to correct my very weak long-distance vision. It was something I had been considering for several years and I had spent many hours researching the topic, speaking to experts, discussing the subject with people who had been through similar experiences and speaking to my wife. Finally, I secured enough money for this elective treatment and went forward.

The procedure at that time was quite remarkable, although I'm sure it has improved considerably in the years since then. After many tests and much analysis, I arrived for my appointment and at the appropriate time was required to lay down on a surgical bed, after which my eye sockets were cleaned, some form of clamp was placed over my right eye, and the cornea was cut to allow a flap to be folded back. The doctor then pointed a laser at me, and I was told to lay still and stare at the red dot, although apparently, the machine reset itself something like 400 times a second to ensure it was aiming at the right place. After 57 seconds on my right eye, the procedure was repeated on my left – this time for only 39 seconds – and then I was good to go.

My vision was a little blurred afterward but by the first evening after the procedure, I could see pretty well out of one eye and, by morning, the sight in both eyes was clear. I had to medicate my eyes with some drops a few times a day and wear ski goggles outside for a week or so to keep dust out, and I had to wear swimming goggles at night to keep me from rubbing my eyes. I had to return three months later to have my right eye slightly adjusted (another seven seconds) to make my vision totally accurate, but the process was an incredible success and when I say life-changing, I mean LIFE–CHANGING.

Why?

I started wearing glasses around the age of seven. At first, I could manage without them for most outdoor activities, but I needed them for school work and had to endure the usual round of offensive and bullying comments. The popular television advertisement for Milky Bars featuring the heroic and bespectacled Milky Bar Kid changed my fortunes somewhat, especially as Karen Marsden in my Grade Three class seemed to like him (and Milky Bars), and she seemed to take a shine to me, too.

As my sporting abilities started to develop, my eyesight became more of a hindrance, and despite the availability of contact lenses, I never found a type that truly worked for me. My main issue was astigmatism in both eyes; both my horizontal and vertical axes had to be aligned, which meant I had to wear what was called toric lenses. These had small grooves in them that were supposed to adjust automatically each time I blinked, allowing the lens to stay in the exact same place to retain clarity of vision. They didn't stay in the same place. And, as a result, my vision was often worse with them than it was without them.

Playing rugby was never easy when I couldn't see the ball as it was kicked towards me, and the odd errant thumb could wipe a lens completely from my eye, resulting in the comical scene of 30 players plus a referee crawling around on their hands and knees looking for a really small piece of plastic amid the mud and dirt.

Cricket was okay, as long as a lens didn't move in my eye – which of course it usually did, especially when I was batting and some fast bowler was about to launch the ball in my direction at some ridiculously fast pace. My lenses were also prone to shifting around when I was fielding and someone hit the ball miles into the air in my direction. The red dot of the ball would be just an incoherent blur coming towards me.

I could get away with wearing my glasses to play golf – until it started raining, after which I couldn't see anything; I also found that my eyes dried up about an hour after I put my lenses in, so a four-hour round of golf was too long to endure the resulting dryness and itching.

It was impossible to wear glasses when I was windsurfing for several reasons, the most important of which was that unless I strapped them on, I was likely to lose them when I'd wipe out, which got very expensive and made it hard to drive home. Being an athletic kind of a guy, my body craved physical activity and yet my vision issues made almost all sporting activities difficult and frustrating, if not downright dangerous.

But the morning after my laser surgery I woke up, sat up, removed my swimming goggles and looked around my bedroom. It was stunning because everything was... *in focus*!

Once my right eye adjustment was complete, and I got approval from my eye surgeon to resume all my regular activities, it was full steam ahead. No more messing with contact lenses before and during rugby matches. No more panicking when batting at cricket and trying to spot a very fast delivery, or looking like a complete idiot in the field. No more craziness trying to put contact lenses in on a windy, sandy beach before heading out on the water, and no more trying to wipe my glasses before every shot on the golf course. I started playing some great rugby, scored more runs and took more catches at cricket. I could windsurf with impunity and my golf handicap improved dramatically.

Why? Simple. It was all about… focus.

## The Wandering Mind Multi-Task Excuse

My wife and I own two cats, *Tommy* and *Grace*, who are named after characters from the TV series *Peaky Blinders*. While they are quite different in personality, they have something in common with pretty much all cats: a low attention span. Either of them may decide to climb on your lap and settle down for a nice nap, but as soon as something attracts their attention – the other cat, a fly, the sound of the food bowl being filled, someone entering through the front door, etc. – they are up and away.

As people get older, our focus similarly starts to wander. Our mind starts to work in mysterious ways. We do things like walk upstairs to fetch something, see something else, do that, then we see something else that needs tending to, we do that and then we return downstairs trying to remember why we went up in the first place.

When we lose focus, our mind tends to fix on what could be wrong, not what could be right, particularly in our Professional Energy Zone. A day that is driven by shallow, insignificant tasks with little or no defined or predictable, useful, outcome is a day wasted and a day that may drain our Physical Energy source while failing to reenergize our Mental Energy.

People think they are expected to multi-task, when in fact other than such activities as walking and eating, it is not possible to multi-task. Instead, we find ourselves *task switching* – leaping from one task to another, without ever committing enough time to focus, never mind achieving any useful work outcome. Many *multi-taskers* devote whole chunks of time to irrelevant tasks that achieve little or nothing. They create the impression they are busy, when in fact they get very small amounts of work completed. And they don't even count their own self–made distractions as being part of the "multi-tasking" domain as they flit from one office task to another and check in on social media several times in the process.

When we get inside an Energy Zone, we have to consider what we want to achieve, why we are there, and how we are going to do it. We need a goal, a routine and a system. This applies to all of our zones, but let's start with our work time. Literally, thousands of books have been written to help people achieve their goals, or become more efficient with their time or learn simple strategies that are guaranteed to make us more productive. But for most people, the answer to achieving all of these objectives is very simple: decide what you need to do – and get on with it.

## Social Media Focus

In Chapter 4 we will discuss the positive as well as the negative impact of Social Media. But one thing that is guaranteed is that it is not going away any time soon. Other than those for whom it is a career, we would probably all prefer to spend less time on Facebook, Instagram, Snap Chat, etc. And, while it does indeed provide a useful vehicle for staying connected to people in a simple format, it is undoubtedly an addiction for many. Not only does it sap our time – try recording how much time you actually spend on Facebook and tell me you are not surprised – but it also destroys our focus. If we allow it to interrupt our work, we then have to refocus to get back to where we were.

I have found that applying the Goals vs. Routines vs. System principle can present a simple solution to the Social Media challenge:

- **Goal** (my "what"): stop allowing Facebook to interrupt my Professional Energy Zone activities.
- **Routine** (my lifestyle or "why"): maintain workflow leading to the timely completion of tasks by not allowing uncontrolled distractions such as social media.
- **System** (the "how"): allow myself a limited amount of time on Facebook each day and reduce that amount of time by a little more each week:
  **Week 1**: 15 minutes – 5 minutes 3 x per day
  **Week 2**: 12 minutes – 4 minutes 3 x per day
  **Week 3**: 10 minutes – 5 minutes 2 x per day
  **Week 4**: 6 minutes – 3 minutes 2 x per day.

**Rules**: select times each day when I will open the Facebook app, then set my timer for the specified time and leave the app when the timer sounds.

When I started using this process, I found that after four weeks it had worked extremely well. It also led to me looking for other activities to do when the timer went off and I had some free time. I might read a newspaper or a book. Consequently, I achieved my goal of stopping Facebook from interrupting my workflow. I am now in control of when I log into Facebook, so I spend less time there. This proves the system worked well, so I can spend more time doing the activities that are important to me.

Let's say it's Monday morning and you are just opening up your workstation to start the week. You may have seen a few emails over the weekend and you probably replied to some of them as well; you have a pretty good idea of what the week ahead of you will look like.

You attend a team "huddle" to get things started and your schedule for the day includes three or four hours of meetings, some of which are routine, and others that are project-specific. Around 15 emails require your attention and another 10 are probably copied to you but do not need a response. You have a "to do" list from Friday that includes six tasks that were not completed, and you have already added another four from the team huddle and the emails you have reviewed. You now have an hour before your first meeting and you clearly have a lot of work to do. But how should you spend that time?

If you look at everything in front of you as a large picture, it will look rather like things did for me before my laser eye surgery: I couldn't see the fastballs. I couldn't see the highballs. I had to keep stopping to wipe the rain off my glasses. I didn't hit the ball cleanly. I either dropped the catches or never got anywhere near them. I couldn't see the green through the raindrops on my glasses. I would get frustrated, I would get angry, I didn't succeed, I didn't achieve very much, I started getting behind and my Mental Energy sources started to deplete before the week had even started.

But, if I can see the ball clearly – no matter how fast it is travelling, or how high it has been hit – there is a much better chance I can hit it or catch it. If I can see the green very clearly through the rain, I have a much better chance of putting the ball on it. And if I do not have to worry about losing a contact lens in the water, I can sail much more efficiently and truly enjoy myself.

There is only one ball in cricket. There is only one ball in rugby. You only play with one ball in golf. You only sail one windsurf board at a time on the water. To successfully connect with the objectives of the sports you are playing, and to achieve a desirable outcome, you have to *focus* on that one object.

Many papers and books have been developed to help people in business prioritize their work and decide where they should focus their time. But, unless there has been a complete breakdown in communication – and I acknowledge that happens a lot more than we care to admit at times – every individual should usually have a good idea of what needs to be done, and by when; it is the actual "doing" part that presents so many challenges.

Going back to our Monday morning, if you have been to the team huddle and taken action on your emails, it should be clear if there is a vital task you are absolutely expected to complete in the hour before your first meeting; if not, then you need to focus on:

- What will create the most impact when it is completed?
- How long will a task take, and can I complete it in the time available?
- Who will be affected if I do not complete a task?
- Who is dependent upon me completing a task?

Of course, you have your "To Do" list leftover from Friday and this probably has a couple of *important* or *urgent* tasks on it – indeed, you have no doubt been using Stephen Covey's tried and tested four-quadrant Time Management Matrix for many years to classify tasks based on urgency, importance and, ultimately, a priority. Most people using this matrix find the Urgent and Important quadrants are always overloaded, while the Not Urgent and Not Important quadrants look fairly bare. You probably start each week with good intentions around your "To Do" list, and you cross off tasks as you proceed through the day, but every morning you transfer the remaining tasks to a new list, add new items and repeat. On Day Three, you take the residue from Day Two (some of which has been passed over since Day One) and repeat. Day Four, same process, you take the residue from Day Three (on which some tasks from Day One still remain) and... you get the idea. We can all recognize that at some point, we look at a task that has been on the list for several days, acknowledge that we are probably just not going to do it and drop it.

Several years ago, I adopted a technique that was a serious game changer for me when determining how to focus my time. It is now a well-known system that many people embrace, and I have been successfully teaching it to the point of getting regular emails from clients who are keen to tell me how much it has changed their lives.

## The ABCs of Focusing Your Time

No more "To Do" lists – okay? Because you are now going to work with an ABC List.

Your A-List items are non-negotiable, *must–get–done–today* tasks. You are not leaving your workplace unless they are done – even if it means you are there until 11:59 p.m. They *absolutely* have to be done today. Does this mean they are important? They might be, or they might not be. BUT you *must* do them today. An A-List task could be something as simple as emptying your garbage bin because it is overflowing and getting a bit smelly, and tomorrow is garbage collection day, and you need to dump it in the main waste area.

It could mean it is your eldest child's birthday tomorrow and you have to return home that evening with a present, *or else*. Is this an important task? Maybe not with regard to the future of your business, but with regard to the future relationship with your child it certainly is.

But most importantly, an A-List task will be work-related and specific to your function in working on routine expectations or projects. "A-List" does not mean *important*, it means *urgent*. When I say it *must be done today* I mean it, because if you *don't* complete an A-List task by the end of the day, and there are no consequences, then it should *never* have even been on the list!

## Milking the Cows

I grew up in Yorkshire in the North of England and although we always lived in or near a town, we were generally surrounded by farmland. I left home at the age of 16 and a few years later my parents moved to the Peak District, a National Park in the county of Derbyshire. Their house has sweeping views of hills and valleys, villages and farmland, and indeed, right across the dry brick wall of their garden are cows and lambs. When I visit my parents, there is hardly an early morning when I don't hear farm noises, or see the cows heading into the barn for the daily milking ritual, and when I say daily, I mean it!

Cows have a fairly simple lifestyle: they eat grass all day and they produce milk. This is a non-negotiable process that has to be supported by the farmer, because, when your cows' udders are full, they have to be emptied. So, if you ever fancy getting into dairy farming, be aware – when it comes to milking the cows, there is no such thing as a day off.

How does this apply to our A-List tasks?

As part of your A-List, there will always be tasks you have to complete every single day. These can be generic tasks such as checking your inbox and taking action on emails (we will cover this in more detail later), filling in daily activity reports, stock taking or ordering products, etc. I like to call these tasks *indelibles*, because they should be permanently on your A-List and completed every day regardless of what else you have to accomplish. You may have to deal with them several times a day, in fact, and you probably don't even need to be reminded to check your inbox. In fact, most people do this way too often or have notification settings that are nothing other than a serious distraction. It is worth being aware that this is a *task*, not a way of life. Check your inbox at certain times, rather than constantly react to it.

One of the major mistakes people make with the principle of the A-List is that they load up too many items and they end up working way too many hours, or they don't complete some tasks, which means, once again, they should not have been added to the list in the first place. You may find yourself with an hour of work time available between meetings and are considering how to spend it. Your A-List is the place to be. Select something that *has* to be done today and crack on with it.

The A-List also has significant benefits from a leadership perspective, because if I want to know where my team members are focusing their time and energy – and I should know this – their A-Lists are where I need to be looking. It gives me a clear picture of what they believe are urgent tasks and if this doesn't align with my own perception, there needs to be some discussion for more clarity; checking in on their A-List also shows me what their capacity is for additional work. Retrospectively, if my boss wants to add work to my schedule, I can use my A-List to display where I am focusing my efforts in an attempt to achieve work balance. I have often been tasked with a last-minute project and when I have explained to

## Tap The Bucket

One technique that has been used for many years to encourage people to get on with tasks and avoid getting entrapped by large projects that can sometimes grind productivity to a halt is called "Tap the Bucket." Imagine you have a bucket that will fit a large rock, a few dozen small stones and half a bag of sand. Your task is to transport the objects in your bucket from Point A to Point B, but nothing is allowed to protrude above the top of the bucket. Most people would start by pouring the sand into the bucket, then adding the small stones and then the large rock – which by now won't fit, as there is not enough room.

Project Failure.

The correct approach is to place the large rock in first, then the smaller stones – which will fill in some of the gaps around the rock – then, finally, the sand. In order to include all of the sand, you may be required to *tap the bucket*, which causes the sand and the small stones to drop further into the bucket, as the jiggling causes the contents to settle. This principle is an excellent analogy for getting through your tasks during the course of a typical day. You have your ABC Lists, for sure, but you will find there are small blocks of time when you may be waiting to head off to a meeting, or you have accomplished an important task and need something quick and easy to do, or maybe you have a set of routine tasks that have been sitting around for too long. By *tapping your bucket*, you just work through a set of those tasks and get them done and out of the way.

my boss what I was currently working on – based on my own assessment of my priorities – he or she has been genuinely surprised. They hadn't quite realized what I was up to and, as a result, they will either defer the additional work or remove some of my objectives.

Another mistake I see quite often with A-List tasks is their lack of specificity. They are too large and not sufficiently clarified.

## Too Much on Your A-List?

I often hear people who have tried and failed with the whole ABC List system complain that there are too many A-List tasks that just don't get done. They go back to the "To Do" list and still don't get around to accomplishing much. An example of where you might run into this could be something like performance evaluations. Say you are responsible for completing 15 staff reports, which could take at least 15 hours, and probably longer if you want to do them properly. This is a very *important* task. I would argue it is probably a leader's *most* important task, but to believe you can complete this in one day is simply not realistic. And yet, I hear people claim it is an A-List task. They have fallen into the *important* versus *urgent* trap again.

Possibly the best way to tackle this would be to divide the evaluations into phases:

Phase 1: Prepare templates for each evaluation

Phase 2: Break the whole group into three rough categories:

- Over-achievers
- Average achievers
- Under-achievers

Phase 3: Draft notes on one category

Phase 4: Draft notes on another category

Phase 5: Draft notes on the final category

Phase 6: Complete each category in full

Then your A-List task today might include Phase 1, and tomorrow it could be Phase 2. Over a period of two weeks, you keep pulling additional Phases from your C-List to your B-List, then pull them into your A-List as you identify a time to complete them.

It should also be noted that other than your indelible tasks, there will be days when your A-List will be empty because there are no tasks that *have* to be done that day, in which case you can focus on, and be selective about, your B-List.

~

Your B-List activities are in some ways more strategic than any others. They are tasks that can be done over the next two or three days, *but* they can also be done *today,* if possible.

B-List tasks have clear deadlines (two or three days away), they are detailed and specific as per the A-List and they will not sit there for a week or more waiting to be tackled. Applying a strategy related to the performance evaluations mentioned above, we could move Phases 2 and 3 to a B-List so they are ready to be moved forward once Phase 1 is complete.

Look at each item on your B-List and ask, *"Can I do this today, and does it HAVE to be done within the next three days?"* If the answer is, "yes" then you are using the system correctly.

~

C-List tasks include everything else that needs to get done at some point in the near future. This may sound like a dump of activity, but there are still some important ground rules. For example, do not add tasks that you recognize are not going to get done. This might include reading the monthly industry magazine that arrives on your desk every four weeks. You know you should probably read it; it may have some useful information for you, but if you don't, then it is not the end of the world. Reading that magazine could be a nice lunchtime activity that would take you away from a screen for an hour, or you could take it home and read it on the train or while on an upcoming business trip. But if you specifically add it to your C-List, then you will simply keep looking at it and scanning over it. Only add C-List items that *have* to be done at some point.

By the way, if you extend this concept to a team environment, change your deadlines so tasks must be completed in a week, then a month, etc., rather than on a day-by-day basis.

/2-

An excellent process to assess how well your ABC strategy is working is to track selected items. If they are flowing nicely from C, through B, and into A, then it's working well. You will always get sudden, unexpected tasks slipping straight onto your A-List, but it is important you consider what actions you could take to alleviate these events and plan them from C forwards.

The whole essence of this theory – and indeed this book – is to *focus your energy in order to get things done*, and your ABC List is a key component of this system.

/2-

Those are some key principles around how to use the ABC List in your Professional Energy Zone.

But how does this apply to our Personal and Social Energy Zones?

Well, pretty much the same principles are at work, to be honest.

You can add a Personal task to your A-List (see above about your eldest child's birthday present), or booking a yoga class or a round of golf. Or you can keep a totally separate list for your Personal Energy Zone activities for a weekend – e.g. completing a run-training workout, washing the car, making a phone call to an elderly relative, etc. And while these tasks may not include any indelibles, they should be focused on key objectives. For me, if I am training for a race, then a Saturday morning workout is probably an A-List task for that day. A yoga class or recovery massage might be a B-List task, and getting my bike into the shop for servicing could be a C-List task.

Social Energy Zones are almost certainly going to involve a group of family and/or friends, and that could revolve around making travel arrangements for a vacation. There may be key timelines that need to be adhered to, and so you need to close out your bookings over the next day or so, hence that could be an A or B List objective.

Now we have a simple, but highly effective system through which we can identify what we should be doing and when.

## Leave It on the Green

We consider factors related to the difference between good and great athletes at various points in this book and one of the components is, of course, mindset. This applies as much – if not more – in golf as it does in any other sport and how a player reacts to a poor hole is particularly instructive. I have had the good fortune to attend many professional golf tournaments over the years and one area that always impresses me is how well the great players leave a bad hole behind.

My general approach to taking a 6, a 7 or worse, on a hole is to try and make up for it off the next tee, which of course usually results in a ridiculously fast swing, a lifting of my head... and the rest does not a happy memory make. But the world's greatest players – who all drop shots at some point – literally leave their thoughts on the green. They clear their mind and focus on the next shot as a new hole, a new beginning and a new opportunity to pull some strokes back. *Focus* is their mantra, their buzz word, their guiding light, and those who can master this area of their game will be very successful players. The same applies to us in any of our Energy Zones. The better able we are to leave any negative thoughts on the last green and look at the next tee as a new opportunity, the more rewarding our time in that zone will be.

## Focus Squares

Focus plays an important part in our ability to learn new skills, or master a particular craft or just get something right. I remember attending a rugby coaching course where we watched a goal kicker practicing scoring penalties. He was a high-quality professional player, but his success rate for kicking goals was only around 75%. The team had brought in a coach to work with him on this particular aspect of his game, and after he had taken a few kicks – of which he missed around 25% as usual – they sat down and chatted. The coach asked the player what his favourite drink was, and did he like one after each training session? The player responded that his favourite drink was Guinness and, yes, he usually had a pint after training.

The coach then set up a simple system that would determine if and when the player would get a Guinness. He drew five squares in a row on a piece of paper with a sketch of a pint of Guinness at the end. The player had to kick the first penalty and if he scored, there would a checkmark in Box 1. He then had to kick again and if he scored a checkmark would go in Box 2, and so on, until he scored five in a row – then he got to go and have his pint of Guinness. But if he missed a kick, he went back a box, and if he missed the next one, he went back again – until he had to start all over again with five empty boxes.

The exercise is quite fascinating because when you have four boxes complete, you only have to score once and you are done – but if you miss, you are back to Box 3, then Box 2. That means your concentration level after four boxes is extremely high. But if you miss, you have to concentrate even harder just to get back to Box 4. This totally changed the kicker's focus and concentration levels and there was a significant improvement in his success rate.

You can adapt this method in many scenarios. If I am learning a script for a presentation, I will buy a block of chocolate that I will only get to eat if I complete the script five times with no errors. As someone who loves chocolate, it seriously makes me focus on the task at hand. I also know many music teachers who use this technique with their pupils when they are learning to play scales (few students like scales, so getting them done is always a prize in itself, even without adding chocolate).

If you want to be capable of focusing on the tasks you need to accomplish – while building and applying an effective system for achieving your goals so you can create the routines of a more rewarding lifestyle – you need to give your mind sufficient stimulation throughout all its waking hours. This will likely result in you feeling more refreshed – with a full Mental Energy Pack – and ready for more of the same the next day. But if you do not have that focus, then you may be allowing yourself to drown for hours in the cesspit of social media and internet addiction. My sporting life changed dramatically once I had laser eye surgery, which for me is a great example of the importance of focus in our lives.

If focus is an issue for you, give your mind a challenging alternative to taking the easy option – that's why I like *Running in the Rain*.

# CHAPTER 4

# Don't Distract Me While I'm Driving

*You can always find a distraction if you are looking for one.*

**–Tom Kite**

Running, in general, is not only a great distraction, it is also a cure for being distracted. *Running in the Rain* enhances that experience by making it a more worthwhile distraction and an even stronger cure to being distracted. A former colleague of mine would never cease to puzzle me with his life and working practices. He was an accomplished distance runner who regularly qualified for major marathons and even won several age-group races. His day always started with a run, often very early to allow him to get to the office for work, and each weekend there would be at least one very long-distance effort. He was highly committed to his training, to the point where taking a rest day, and taking time off to recover from an injury, were difficult for him to handle. His training hours were a key part of his life and they were scheduled into pretty much every day, no matter where he was in the world or what the weather was like.

But what I found interesting about my experience of working with him, was his general behaviour around the office and how it differed from his approach to running. At work, he was almost permanently reactive to his phone, email or text. He would sit in meetings and constantly text people or check his email; he scrolled through websites and was generally thoroughly distracted to the point where he would often miss a question thrown his way.

My colleague's job was not customer – or supplier – facing, so few immediate action tasks ever required him to react; instead, it seemed his phone addiction was purely self-inflicted. If I was out for lunch with him, he would stop mid-sentence to respond to the buzzing of his phone and he had no qualms about answering it if I were talking. The same applied in his office during meetings, no matter who was talking. On one occasion when he came to meet with me and some other members of the team, I asked everyone to turn off their phones while in my office. He reluctantly complied, but he became increasingly anxious as time passed until he excused himself for a bathroom break, during which I can only imagine he checked in online.

As a close friend of the CEO, he was pretty much allowed free rein, but his work behaviour was so governed by distractions that he was *the* biggest distraction in the company. Ironically, when asked whether he stopped to check his messages while running, he laughed and said nothing could ever distract him from his training. But by allowing himself to be distracted in the office, he became a huge distraction for everyone else.

## The Role of the Subthalamic Nucleus

When human beings encounter something unexpected, a brain system called the Subthalamic Nucleus (STN) engages, causing the person to make an abrupt stop so they can observe and react quickly to the potential threat they're facing. The STN is a small lens-shaped part of the brain and from a functional point of view, it is a component of the basal ganglia system. The STN not only causes you to physically make an abrupt stop, but it also causes your mind to abruptly halt *all* thought so it can focus on the potential threat it's facing.

Imagine you are driving along a country road on a beautiful summer's day. You are singing along to a song on the radio or chatting with family members who are in the car with you, and all is well in your world. Then, out of the corner of your eye, you see a car approaching the next intersection along a side road to your right. It is travelling very quickly and doesn't appear to be slowing down. In fact, as you get closer to the intersection, the driver of the other car has to slam on his brakes to avoid driving out in front of you. By now you have moved your foot from the gas pedal to the brake and you are ready to steer around this idiot should they fail to stop. But what else has happened? You have stopped singing along to the radio or chatting with your fellow travellers. What caused this to happen?

Well, we know that the danger of a car driving out in front of us stopped our singing or chatting, but this was caused by the STN triggering the closure of current focus in order to deal with a threat or distraction. This is an important part of our brain's function and it protects us.

But it doesn't stop there.

If you carry on driving and another car almost pulls out in front of you, the STN reacts again and shuts down the current focus, but then, it starts to take over your mind because it is now on constant alert for the next event, which makes refocus on the original task even harder. If there aren't any repeats of the distraction, after a while there will be withdrawal symptoms, making it even harder to truly work at the original level of focus. In other words, you start to become disappointed if there are no further dangers, as you are ready and waiting for them.

With our modern society so full of interruptions, the STN triggers the same thought-halting effect for any interruption, regardless of whether it's a danger to us or not. This means it can be nearly impossible to focus on a task at hand.

Why are distractions becoming more damaging to our lifestyle? Aren't they simply part of the fabric of our existence? Part of modern society? Akin to the increased dangers of travel as people invented faster cars? Well, the truth is that distractions can occur no matter what Energy Zone we are in and the impact can be just as damaging in our Professional, Personal or Social Zones.

As a knowledge worker, someone can be constantly harassed by a barrage of distracting events that never seem to stop for more than a few seconds.

When we are in our Personal Energy Zone trying for some evening downtime to read a book or complete a Netflix series, there are seemingly constant distractions that break our concentration. And even when we are enjoying our Social Energy Zone activities with family and friends, there will be something that interrupts the occasion and dilutes the zone.

The implications can be huge. Our work drags on longer every day and week, we end up rushing tasks – or just putting them off in the hope no one notices – or we end up burning out through working some crazy long hours. We get little fulfillment from our *me* time as we are constantly pulled away, meaning we never truly disengage from the events of the world we are often trying to escape; the family unit becomes more and more damaged due to the erosion caused by distractions and the effect they have on us and those close to us.

## Distractions: The Impact

Most people are aware that distractions impact their work and personal lives, but let's take a closer look at some of the facts.

A 2012 McKinsey study found the average knowledge worker spends 60% of the workweek engaged in electronic communication and Internet searching, with close to 30% of a worker's time dedicated to reading and answering email alone.

During his first term in office, Barack Obama hired Tom Cochran as his Chief Digital Strategist tasked with working with his team in the White House and Department of State. Cochran went on to take up the position as Chief Technology Officer at *Atlantic Media* during which time he produced a research essay for the *Harvard Business Review* in 2012 entitled "Email Is Not Free."

Cochran was keen to point out that his job description did not include managing email flow and very few knowledge worker job descriptions do. He went on to assess the impact of managing his workflow around email and calculated that each week he would receive an average of 511 inbound emails. He would send 284 outbound emails, which amounts to almost 160 emails per day, and 235 of those were internal emails from people in his department; 172 were CCs with no action required from him other than reading them. There was an average of 32 words per email, and most were superfluous update emails with no value. Cochran also calculated that each individual email ate up 95 cents' worth of labour costs, which, when totalled up, meant the labour costs of managing email for one year in *Atlantic Media* was equivalent to the purchase of a Lear Jet.

In 2018, *RescueTime* CEO, Robby Macdonell, reported the results of a study into the impact of email and Instant Messaging tools (such as Slack) on workplace productivity. The report claims this form of communication has changed from being a help to being a hindrance. His study found that 84% of email users keep their inboxes open in the background at all times and 70% of all emails are opened within six seconds of receipt. Staff members have become proficient at being responsive, but they have sacrificed the ability to do their best work. Much of our most important work requires deep focus and time to think. *Always-on* communication technology requires workers to respond and, in so doing, steals the precious resource of focus leaving employees frustrated about not accomplishing "real work."

Macdonell asked the question: is email and communication technology really that bad?

To find out, *RescueTime* looked at the anonymized worldwide data of more than 50,000 knowledge workers and found a trend of distraction and interruption in the workplace that was worse than they expected. Knowledge workers – like writers, designers, developers and project managers – depend on collaboration and quick access to information to meet the demands of their roles.

Communication tools facilitate getting the information needed, but they are also a constant source of interruption to focused work. When the *RescueTime* team looked at the data, they found that the average knowledge worker "checks in" with communication tools every six minutes. (They defined a "check-in" as any time you switch to a communication tool while working on another productive task.)

How can business leaders expect employees to accomplish focused work when they only have a few minutes in-between answering emails and messages in which to do so? The short answer is that it cannot be done.

As the *RescueTime* team looked at the full breakdown, the picture became even bleaker. According to their study, 35% of workers checked their email and Instant Messages every three minutes or less, while only 18% were able to go more than 20 minutes without being pulled into communication. Also, the team found that people who use the Slack app – a tool intended to reduce email traffic – actually switched communication tools more often. Rather than streamlining their communication time, Slack users on average spent only five minutes in between communication check-ins, while non-Slack users could go eight minutes.

The conclusion? Technology that is being used to ostensibly improve work is actually hurting people's ability to get work done. The constant communication interruptions are not only diminishing productivity but also keeping workers from doing their best work and growing in their careers. *RescueTime's* data showed that 40% of knowledge workers never get 30 minutes of straight focused time in a workday. In fact, the study revealed that 40 minutes was the longest stretch most people went without checking email in a day. That means that nearly half of knowledge workers rarely get time for focused work.

## Productivity Study in New Zealand

In July 2018, *The New York Times* reported on a productivity experiment a New Zealand company did when they switched to a four-day, 32-hour workweek. According to the company, workers reported that the change motivated them to find ways to be more productive while in the office. Meetings went from two hours in length to 30 minutes and employees created signals for their colleagues to indicate they needed time to work without distraction.

The key outcomes of the New Zealand study suggest strategies that all organizations can apply with or without a 4-day work week, that is if they can allow themselves to focus without distractions, productivity increases.

## Communications Batching

Many productivity experts have suggested batching communications into specific blocks during the day, while others have suggested committing to an hour or more of focused work without email or Instant Messaging (IM) during parts of the day when you're less likely to be needed. The modern workplace is filled with distractions and as organizations work to improve productivity the disruptive nature of communication tools is often overlooked. Email and IM in the workday are here to stay, but how they are managed and utilized requires some considerable changes in approach. Being aware of the distraction can help us all find a better balance, which will improve productivity and assist us to feel more in control of our energy and so master our time. To this end, we need to consider how to be more disciplined with our communication tools, which may require shifting the expectations of those with whom we communicate and setting realistic priorities.

The data outlined in all of the studies above very clearly highlight an urgent need to regain focus and not allow communication tools to rob our productivity or digital wellness. Furthermore, during a recent series of extended workshops my company delivered to a number of organizations, we focused on the implications of distractions and the major causes. Our discussions discovered that more than 90% of participants held *themselves* in some way accountable for the distractions that interrupt their work and of these distractions, email, instant messaging, and social media were the most significant culprits. Furthermore, when we analyzed who most often transmitted messages where hasty responses were expected, the fingers were pointed almost unanimously at participants' managers.

Email and Instant Messaging has proven to be the Number One distraction for all of our Energy Zones, and we will explore the specifics of how to better deal with them in Chapter 6. For now, we'll put it on our list of common distractions.

In 2018, Udemy published a *Workplace Distraction Report* in which they recorded that 75% of workers felt they would be more productive if distractions in the workplace were reduced. Their sources quoted a joint study from the University of California, Irvine, and the Institute of Psychology, Humboldt University, Berlin, in which the ability of participants to reorient to a task once they had been interrupted was assessed. The scenarios were broken down into three categories:

- Distraction by a task similar to the one being performed at the time.
- Distraction by a task unrelated to the original task being performed.
- A constant mixture of the above.

Researchers concluded that no matter the source or subject of the interruption, the time to reorient to the original task was the same, but work became hurried, stress levels increased and the quality of work decreased. The results also suggested that interruptions lead people to change not only work rhythms but also strategies and mental states.

Udemy reported that millennials and Gen Zs spend around two hours per day checking their devices and an average of 62% of all workers spend at least an hour per day using their phones for non-work-related activity.

The lines are also becoming increasingly blurred between personal and work activities and the Number One overall techie distraction is Facebook (65%).

## Social Media – The Modern Addiction

Returning to the road trip we discussed earlier in our exploration of the Subthalamic Nucleus (STN), imagine that instead of driving along a country road you are working on your laptop on an important project and in place of a dangerous driver about to pull out in front of you, your phone announces a Social Media notification. Your STN kicks in and closes down your project focus to deal with the interruption. If you then return to work and your phone buzzes again, your STN will then go on constant alert waiting for the next notification. And if there is a slight pause in interruptions, there will be withdrawal symptoms (why haven't they replied to my last comment? Did I offend someone?).

Does this sound familiar?

It isn't too difficult to argue for the benefits of Social Media, because for someone like me, who immigrated to North America from the United Kingdom (UK) in 2005, it is an efficient method to keep in touch with old friends and former colleagues without having to write emails or letters or make regular transatlantic phone calls. My elderly parents are also able to observe events involving many of my activities, as well as those of my friends, who they know well.

There are many essays written on the subject of Social Media addiction, many of which state defending social media usage should be based on either identifying any possible benefits of its use or pointing out what would be missing if it wasn't used. Many people claim we would probably be better off without it.

Addiction is a strong word, but it's often accurate when applied to many people's practices in this area; rather than eliminating it completely, it is surely true that its use requires careful management. A client in one of my programs recently admitted that while his job required him to check in on LinkedIn daily, rather than spending the minimum amount of time completing his responsibilities, he would become distracted with an article or set of comments and, without noticing, could spend more than an hour scrolling through indeterminate material with no beneficial outcome. While LinkedIn may have a stronger case for claiming our attention while in our Professional Energy Zone than, say, Facebook or Instagram, any form of social media that is not carefully controlled will quite simply control us.

How many times have we been in our Personal Energy Zone and while attempting to sit and read a book or pay attention to a TV show, we react to our phone buzzing with a Facebook notification?

How many times has a family sat around the dinner table when a teenager has been pulled out of the Social Energy Zone and into their Personal Zone with a Snapchat notification?

Some potential practices that may be adopted with regard to Social Media outcomes were discussed in Chapter 3, but for the benefit of dealing with our distraction issue, let's just add it to the list of what we face seemingly throughout all our Energy Zones.

## Time to Circle the Wagons

K. Anders Ericsson was a Florida State University academic researcher who claimed in a 1990s paper that *deliberate practice* is the essence of high undistracted performance. He argued that the differences between expert performers and normal adults reflect a life-long period of a *deliberate effort* to improve performance in a specific domain. This refers back to my comments in Chapter 2 regarding great versus average athletes: great athletes are better able to deal with the boredom of continual training practices in a more positive way, and that makes them better. The essence of the lifestyle to which we want to subscribe is:

- to be more productive.
- to get our tasks done so we can get on with the fun stuff.
- to feel like we have achieved something.
- to create endorphins (preferably not to keep us awake, but rather to stimulate our Mental Energy Pack).

None of this will happen if we are constantly distracted out of our zone.

As we consider a strategy to overcome distractions, let's ponder the following:

*In order to produce a high level of performance, we need to create a space where there is a defined amount of focused time, during which we will complete a specific task or series of tasks.*

Returning to our Goals vs. Routines vs. System principle, let's consider this:

- Goal (my what): To alleviate distractions in order to be more productive in my Professional Energy Zone.
- Routine (my lifestyle or why): To lead a distraction-free professional life so I can spend more time on the tasks that are important to me.
- System (my how): Create some form of sanctuary in order to block myself off from distractions and allow me to work freely.

30 Day System Test: After 30 days I need to ask if I have alleviated distractions in order to be more productive in my Professional Energy Zone.

- Yes?: The system is working.
- No?: The system not working – change is required.

What's this about a sanctuary, you ask? Stay tuned, we'll be looking at that in more detail in the next chapter.

# CHAPTER 5

# I'm Trying to Work Here

*Productivity is never an accident. It is always the result of a commitment to excellence, intelligent planning and focused effort.*

**–Paul J. Meyer**

*unning in the Rain* is like being in my own personal sanctuary. I see fewer runners than usual and those I do see nod in a way that suggests we are bound by the commitment to overcoming the adversity of the rain to get out and run.

Let's consider this *sanctuary* thought then for a moment. It is defined as a *place of refuge or safety*, and wouldn't that be a nice place to be in order to reduce distractions, focus on our work and complete the tasks that are important to us?

In 2014 I was working on a coaching program[5] with a technology company in Toronto that had recently moved into new premises. When I say "new," I mean the office was new to them but quite old (in a

---

[5] If you would like to find out more about the kind of assistance my team and I might be able to lend your organization, I invite you to check out our services at **andrewjane.com**. For specific information about working free from distractions, go to **distractionfreedom.com**.

Canadian sense). The CEO was insistent on creating an open-plan office in which the whole staff of around 150 would *"work without walls."* He was a huge fan of Mark Zuckerberg and was interested in the Facebook office in Silicon Valley that housed over 2,500 staff in one room. My client's theory was based around his need for a team – and – togetherness environment and he and all his senior leadership team were set up with workstations in long lines of desks along with everyone else. They had created several glass-walled office spaces alongside the main floor that served as meeting rooms, but the general idea was that it was "one for all and all for one" in the main space.

I had my reservations regarding how this was going to work, and these were realized around three months after they were up and running when I asked my client how things were working out. The CEO replied that while the theory was good, and the atmosphere was very positive with everyone working in this big happy family room, the practicalities were not so great, because his team was finding the environment less than conducive to focused work – in other words, there was too much noise and people couldn't concentrate when trying to complete important projects.

We talked about a few options. In the company's previous location, we had created some effective closed-door policies that had allowed his team limited periods of time to work uninterrupted. We also considered how we could replicate an outward "Do Not Interrupt" message system to allow people to work alone on key tasks.

We started by handing out company baseball caps that staff could wear if they wanted to be left alone to focus on key work, but some people didn't want to wear a hat in the office. We then tried using the luminous vests that construction workers wear on the open roads, but while that appeared more popular, there was still too much noise. Some people tried a pair of high-quality noise-canceling headphones but even then they had to listen to music, which not everyone found practical. There were still too many distracting sounds that reduced the opportunity to focus and get work done effectively.

It got so bad that some staff would call in sick just so they could stay home and work in peace and quiet to complete a project, and one guy would sometimes disappear and go and sit in his car in the parking lot so he could work without distraction. Furthermore, many staff members were young graduates who lived locally and other than working, they had few commitments in life, so they tended to work very long hours as they had little else to do. It didn't help that if someone worked past 8:00 p.m. they got a free meal voucher. The CEO recognized that this lifestyle was going to lead to burnout, plus, at some point, those younger team members would start settling down and starting families, after which they would soon stop working such long hours. He ultimately wanted to put a ban on anyone working after 5:30 p.m., but he realized this could have significant implications on productivity.

So, we came up with an idea we called *Dark Zones*.

Most of the staff arrived in the office by 8:30 a.m. and this allowed them 30 minutes to start up their workstation, get a coffee, have a quick team huddle, and define their workflow for the morning. Everyone was expected to have a clear idea of what their A-List tasks were for the day, and what they were going to focus on first. We invested in small desk lamps for each team member and blinds for the windows. At exactly 9:00 a.m., the blinds were closed, the main lights were lowered, the desk lights were switched on and the *Dark Zone* started.

There were some associated *Dark Zone* rules that went with this strategy:

1. There was to be no talking and if someone had to answer an important external phone call, they would step into one of the meeting rooms.

2. No internal emails were to be sent during the *Dark Zone* period, other than those categorized as *critical*. [6]

---

[6] See Chapter 6 for more on email discipline.

3. If there were a corporate crisis that needed immediate attention, then whoever was involved would immediately convene in a meeting room. (In reality, once strict rules were applied and the clear definition of "crisis" confirmed, this hardly ever happened.)

4. Notifications were turned off on all phones with the exception of text messages, which were only used for critical communication. In other words, if your phone buzzed, then it should only be a critical text message.

5. No Social Media was allowed, either on phones or PCs.

6. Staff were allowed to respond to personal texts if they were related to a personal emergency.

At the end of the *Dark Zone* period, the main lights were switched back on and employees resumed their normal office activities. Routine, Operational, and Reference emails were dispatched and some in-person ad-hoc meetings were convened to discuss any immediate routine or project issues.

We started with a 20-minute block of time for the first week of *Dark Zone* practise, then increased it to 30 minutes, 45 minutes, and then to an hour. After a 3-month trial period, it was decided that 45 minutes was the optimal period and so every day, four blocks of *Dark Zone* time were executed at 9:00 a.m., 10:30 a.m., 2:00 p.m., and 3:30 p.m., except on Fridays, when POETS day rules[7] were applied and only two blocks of *Dark Zone* time were required.

The results were impressive. The CEO estimated productivity increased by at least 40%, meaning he could deliver to his customers within a shorter time frame. Staff appeared more energized and he was able to apply his *"Stop work at 5:30 p.m."* rule. His Human Resources department noticed a significant increase in employee satisfaction ratings, as well as an increase in staff retention, particularly in the critical 28 – 35 age

---

[7] Push Off Early Tomorrow's Saturday

groups that so many tech companies rely on for consistent evolution and business growth. Additional benefits included an increase in bottom-line profits, which were pumped back into the company to increase research and development, and they were able to award each employee an additional week of vacation per year.

## Let's Talk about Focus Zones

*Dark Zones* are not going to suit all companies but there are few reasons why teams and individuals cannot apply a similar strategy. And I have found it generally more productive to talk about *Focus Zones* rather than *Dark Zones* in exploring the idea of creating a sanctuary where people can complete tasks undisturbed. One client recently noted that she does this by imagining a desert island on which she is a castaway with no internet, no phone and no people to interrupt or distract her.

## The Physical Space

What will your physical *Focus Zone* space look like?

For some, it may be a small office space with a *Do Not Disturb* sign on the door. It may mean simply being allowed to work from home. I know a CEO who likes to fly long–haul business class flights, a stopover for a few hours, then return, because no one can distract him while he is in the air.

There is a Starbucks coffee shop close to my home that for some reason won't allow me to connect to their wi-fi, so if I turn my phone off as well, I can be completely offline while I sit and work. I have found this to be one of the most productive places for me to work, even when there are lots of distractions with customers coming and going – in fact, I often get more work done there than in my home office. I also enjoy business travel and I have found sitting in a hotel lobby in the evening to be a particularly great place to work.

Some people like to simply go for a walk to let thoughts percolate in their minds and I have business associates who will never make a key decision until they have taken a couple of showers, as they often think of things in that environment that they do not think of at any other time. Ultimately it does not really matter what your *Focus Zone* space physically looks like – as long as you can function there without distraction.

## Send a Signal

It's good to remember that when we create a *Focus Zone* we can't assume that everyone else on the planet knows we are there and should not disturb us. I have heard countless clients tell me their boss expects them to be available at all times. When I ask them if their boss would object if they told them they were going to be offline for 45 minutes in order to complete an important task, no one has ever said they felt this would be a problem. In fact, some teams have sent group emails to their bosses with a request for *Focus Zone* solitude between, for example, 10:30 – 11:15 a.m. to finish *Project X*. This is simply a basic version of the *Dark Hours* concept. Several people have told me their bosses thought this was a good idea and had encouraged the whole team to block time each day precisely for that purpose. Even encouraging others to work in parallel with us can be contagious and I always get a warm feeling when I hear that more members of a team are adopting the *Focus Zone* principles.

Most of us set our automated *Out of Office* email response if we are away on vacation or at a conference, or generally travelling, but how many people set it each day for the specific times they need to focus on a task rather than be disturbed? There are numerous reports available that claim exorbitant amounts of money are lost each year by businesses due to distractions in the workplace, and unfocused and interrupted staff leads to increased employee dissatisfaction, which probably leads to even more distractions as people do "more interesting things than work." So why not take 30 seconds to update your *Out of Office* message when you head into your *Focus Zone* and explain that you are not available for the next 45 minutes? You can advise people that you will respond to emergencies communicated by text on your phone... and then turn off all phone notifications other than text.

## Focus Zone Communications

We will look more at email communication management tools later, but one of the reservations many people have is that they will feel something akin to loneliness if they are disconnected from their email for any length of time. As discussed earlier, many studies reveal people react to most emails within a few seconds, which suggests they are becoming almost totally *reactive* in their daily working routines. This is creating a culture of connectivity guided by the false rule that we have to reply *now*. In fact, the more "responsible" you are around replying to email the greater the expectation will be for you to take action. And the more email traffic you will receive.

Why do we get hooked into the endless vacuum of reactive communications?

Because it is easier.

We start an email exchange to try to solve a problem without realizing the impact it will have on the other party or parties. This can be selfish and demoralizing when the time spent in meetings may be far more constructive. Forwarding an email to a group of colleagues with the subject line, "What do you think?" only takes a few seconds, but can then lead to many minutes – if not hours – of distracted time spent in response, much of which will be ignored anyway.

By contrast, how many emails could a three minute conversation between four people save?

Some companies develop detailed strategies for prioritizing workflow, then send a continual barrage of emails to their staff, expecting them to live in this focus-deprived world of reactive communication. And then they berate people for getting behind on their work!

Remember, the vast majority of staff blame their managers for being one of the main sources of communication distraction in their daily work. This is generally because they feel their manager is expecting a response immediately, when in fact there may not be any expectation of the sort. But there may have been no indication of the manager's timeline in the original email. Stating something as simple as, "bring your thoughts to the meeting on Friday," can keep employees from getting stuck in a reactive state and will also prevent a distracting email from being sent back to the manager.

One of the challenges of modern technology is real-time messaging – the ability to continually connect with colleagues at any point in the working day – and evenings, weekends, vacation time, etc. But there has not been much thought put into the negative impact this has on workflow and focus. When we enter our *Focus Zone*, we need to set strong boundaries to protect our space and this comes down to our mindset. Do we *have* to respond *now*? What is the worst possible outcome if we wait even 30 minutes? Does the sender need some space or are they demanding a response? A world dominated by your inbox is not a nice place to live and so it is important that we create some rules to keep our *Focus Zone* protected while we are in it:

- Turn phone notifications off (other than text messages).
- Set *Out of Office* notifications for the period you are in your *Focus Zone* and request only important texts to your phone.
- Switch your computer to Airplane mode.
- Store emails for transmission once you exit your zone (that way you do not need to go back online and become immediately distracted by inbound email).
- Let key people know you are heading into your *Focus Zone* and request that they not disturb you.

## Have a Clear Objective

Back to goals again (yes, they still stink): as we've mentioned earlier, allocating time and tasks to our *Focus Zone* makes life more fun. Opting for a structured system – rather than operating in a world of loose free time where nothing is truly defined or accomplished – is important so that we create some depth of work and a sense of achievement

Our A and B Task lists should *feed* our *Focus Zone*, but we need to be very specific about what we want to achieve, rather than "as much as possible in the time available." As with any new process, it is worth starting small and growing from there. If you were to start meditating for the first time in your life it is unlikely you would manage more than a few minutes at a time and the same applies here. Set yourself a time target (e.g. 10 minutes to begin) and a single task you know you should be able to accomplish in that time frame. Apply the rules, set your timer and proceed. Ensure you are aware of what the successful outcome of the task will look like so you can measure how effective you were. Then increase your time and your expectations. In reality, it is unlikely you will spend more than 45 minutes in your *Focus Zone* at any one time, so large projects will need to be broken down into smaller chunks,[8] otherwise, you will probably procrastinate and break the zone.

## The Tool Kit

One of the benefits of living in North America rather than the UK is the comparative difference in house sizes. For roughly the same price, I was able to buy a house in Canada that was double the square footage of my previous house in England. I have a large basement (in which I have proudly fitted out a workshop), and a double garage, in which there is more storage room for tools, benefits of which many of my British friends can only dream. However, these luxuries come with a downside in that I have to decide where to keep my tools (or else buy double of everything), and you can guarantee that if I am working on something in the garage in the summer, a specific tool will be in the basement and vice versa if working in the basement in winter.

I recently built a very large wooden vegetable garden box in which my wife can grow fresh produce, and while I managed to bring most of the tools I needed from the basement into the garden for the day I was at work, I left three separate tools behind, which caused me (three times) to

---

[8] See Chapter 8 for overcoming Procrastination.

pause, head back inside, unlace and remove my muddy work boots, walk through the kitchen, answer a question about something, go into the basement, see something else I meant to do that morning, do it, collect the missing tool, return upstairs, answer another question, put my boots back on and resume work.

Each break I had to take to get the tools I had forgotten cost me around 20 minutes of production time.

The same applies when we head into our *Focus Zone*. If we do not have everything we need, we will be forced back out and the spell is broken. If you need an attachment from an email, ensure you download it first because if you don't, you will have to go back online and open the dreaded inbox – which will likely suck you into more reactive emails, and when you respond, you will tell people you are out of your zone and available for communication. Other parts of our toolkit can include water or coffee, a project file, any reference notes that are in the *cloud*, a laptop charger, calculator,[9] and basically *anything* we need to ensure we do not have to leave the *Focus Zone*.

## When And For How Long?

As mentioned before, I am often asked how I find time to train for events such as Ironman Triathlons and other endurance sports. After all, I run a business, I have a fairly active family and social life, I like Netflix and Amazon Prime, I love to read, I occasionally play golf, I enjoy windsurfing and I like to travel.

The answer once again, though, is fairly simple. I don't find time to train – I *schedule* it.

Each week I know how many miles I need to put into my swimming, cycling, and running, and how many hours these activities will take. As I approach peak week, the commitment becomes greater, and then it

---

[9] You may have become accustomed to relying on the calculator on your phone – but be aware, by using this in your Focus Zone, you might become distracted by opening up some apps.

starts to ease down. But while I am in command of my own schedule, there are a couple of factors that restrict complete training freedom: the swimming pool opening times and the weather. Lane swims are the only time a serious athlete can get into the pool to train effectively and these are usually scheduled for the early mornings (around 5:30 a.m. – 7:30 a.m.), so I need to ensure I plan my time accordingly. With regard to the weather, while I don't have an issue with *Running in the Rain* (obviously), I prefer not to take my rather expensive triathlon bike out in inclement conditions and cover it with the mud that washes onto the road from the farmlands around where I live. Consequently, my scheduling is based on these two factors, but most importantly, I need to know what I am going to do and when.

The same applies to getting into our *Focus Zones*.

If we try to jump in at random, it will probably work as well as if I decide I will go for a two-hour bike ride sometime on Wednesday… if I have time and the weather's nice and I don't have too much to eat at lunch. In other words, I am fooling myself if I think I will actually get it done.

We briefly looked at what I call the *meditational* approach to *Focus Zone* time commitment earlier when I noted you should probably start with short periods of *Focus Zone* time and extend them, rather than start with a block of 45 minutes. Say I am alone and want to complete a task – it could be simply proofreading a blog or newsletter I have been writing, which would normally take around 20 minutes. I would still head into my *Focus Zone*, switch everything off, set my timer – so I would just get in, get it done and get out – and then crack on.

When we are planning our *Focus Zone* time, we need to be aware of when our "Hot Hours" are. In other words, the times when we are at our most productive. For some people, this may be early in the day, and I have met many people over the years who like to get into the office first thing so they can get some important projects completed when it is quiet. Others like to head into their *Focus Zone* during lunchtime while the office is quieter; still, others are very happy to leave key tasks until later in the day – again, when the office is quiet. Personally, I have found that I am at my most productive just before lunch and then just before I plan to close things down at the end of the day.

Depending on my ABC List, there will be days when I have a routine day of tasks ahead of me that will not be affected too much by distractions and so I do not need to go into my *Focus Zone*. On other days I may feel I need to set aside up to four *Focus Zone* blocks in order to complete an urgent project, do some firefighting, or work on an immediate recovery plan for a client. But these are usually rare occurrences.

## Lay Out Your Kit

We have identified when our *Focus Zone* will be established. We have put up our metaphorical *Do Not Disturb Sign*. We have set up our communications boundary. We have a clear objective of what we want to achieve. We have all the tools we need. We have a start and a finish time – but we are still reticent about jumping in.

Why?

Maybe we worry our team will struggle without us for the next 45 minutes.

Maybe the world will come to a stop while we are zoned off.

Maybe our team will feel cut off and alienated while we are away.

Imagine you are planning to go for a run. You look outside and it is raining, but you know you need to run today. The urge to turn your attention to something more superficial can start to take over. You mess around with your shoes, you check to ensure the back door is closed, you do one more bathroom visit, you check your email on your phone, you check to ensure the refrigerator door is closed… in fact, you dither around rather than get out into the rain because you have a finite amount of willpower that becomes depleted as you use it.

The same applies to entering our *Focus Zones* and it often requires the setting up of rituals to ensure we get going. For me, I commit to my morning training schedule the evening before by laying out my shorts, shirt, socks and shoes (and I add in lots more kit during a Canadian winter). If I'll be swimming the next day then my bag is packed and left by the front door; if it's a cycling day, I even put my bike in the front hallway. This means that should I fail to train, then I have to endure the shame of returning everything unused and deal with the disappointment that generates throughout the day.

By committing to *Focus Zone* times each day to accomplish our tasks, we are effectively *laying out our kit*, and if we fail to proceed, then unless there is some significant extenuating circumstance – which needs to be reviewed to assess whether it can be controlled in future – then we will have to deal with the shame of *Focus Zone Failure*.

## The Exit Strategy

As with any project or practice, the review stage is usually the most overlooked component of using a *Focus Zone* strategy and yet it is probably one of the most important aspects of it. On exiting my *Focus Zone*, I usually assess whether it functioned well. Was I distracted at some point? This can happen even though I have been practising this technique for many years, and it is often because there was something else percolating away in the back of my mind, while I was focused on a specific task, which had taken over. When this happens, I will note that next time I may need to take action to clear the secondary thought first.

If someone has ignored my request for solitude during my *Focus Zone* by physically interrupting me, then that probably means I have not clearly communicated my requirements, or they may have been unclear on what constitutes an emergency. Either way, it is incumbent upon me to clarify.

What happens if the exit review of my *Focus Zone* shows I did not allocate enough time for completing the task? That likely means I took on too much and would need to be more specific next time. I will insert a placeholder in my work and then define another *Focus Zone* as soon as it's convenient, depending on the urgency of the task.

If I finished the task earlier than expected – which happens often – I'll note whether I slid into another task for which I had all the tools at hand or exited into other work with some endorphins in tow.

And finally: were any of the reservations I may have had prior to entering my *Focus Zone* realized? Was the team able to function effectively while I was away? Did I lose any multi-million dollar deals? Did production grind to a halt? Did the world end?

All of these are highly unlikely and so maybe it is time to stop the hesitation and jump straight in. Probably the ultimate coaching question is: what would you change next time? And although we generally do this automatically, it is worth applying as we develop the *Focus Zone* routine and hopefully, these thoughts represent a reasonable starting point.

## Choose Your Reward

The greatest aspect of success is the reward, which can take the form of something significant or something small. My Achilles Heel is chocolate. I love the stuff, but it doesn't love my waistline. However, a couple of squares of something particularly delightful is a fair return for a job well done, a task completed, or a goal secured... and it serves to prove my system is working.

I often ask clients what their personal reward is for the successful completion of a task, and many can't think of anything, although they often admit to eating chocolate during the day. When we turn this into a reward, they see double the benefits. But a reward could be something simple, such as a check-in on social media, a visit to the coffee shop next door, a walk around the block, a favourite website visit, or a few pages of the book you are reading – anything you can do to feel inspired by the endorphins you have just created while ensconced in your *Focus Zone*. And rewards encourage repeat performances – so once you set them up, you will more readily embrace your *Focus Zones* as part of your daily routine.

I have practiced the *Focus Zone* principles for many years and am always happy to share them[10] with people who feel that distractions are really impacting their workflow, their quality of life, and, sometimes, unfortunately, their mental health. But I also hear many people claim they know how to "block off time" to get jobs done, but who actually fail at the task because they do not follow the process identified here. They can't turn off their emails, they don't send a "do not disturb" signal out to others and therefore keep getting interrupted, they don't gather their tools so then they have to go to their inbox to recover an attachment – where they get distracted again – and they don't focus on a specific task. Rather, they just *do some work* in the hope they will actually achieve something. But they don't give themselves a reward because, "well, you know, it was just 30 minutes with my door closed." (Except, it was opened physically or metaphorically at least five times).

While *Running in the Rain* is a great distraction as well as a cure for distraction, *Focus Zones* fall into the same category.

They provide a unique environment with a clear *Do Not Disturb* signal – after all, who is going to run alongside us getting soaked just to bug us about something? While we are *Running in the Rain* we will not be communicating with anyone, we have a clear objective – an amount of time or the distance of the run – and we have the right tools, in this case, wet-weather clothes. We have also committed to a start time with a ritual attached (laying out our kit and defining our preferred training time). And most importantly, when we complete that rain run or exit our *Focus Zone*, we deserve a well-earned reward.

---

[10] For more information on our program to help you overcome distractions, visit www.distractionfreedom.com.

# CHAPTER 6

# I'm Not Ignoring You, I'm Doing Something More Important

*Wise men speak because they have something to say.*
*Fools, because they have to say something.*

**– Plato**

*I* own a great set of headphones that I use when I am either cycling or running. They are "bone conductors" that sit around my head and the speaker is just to the front of each ear, meaning nothing is inserted into my ears. They are very comfortable, and the sound quality is excellent. They are also a safe addition to my training technology: they allow me to hear any passing cars as well as whatever is playing on my phone and they are water-resistant, so I can use them when I am *Running in the Rain*. There is a multi-function button on the left speaker which is easy to operate if I want to pause what I am listening to, or if I have an incoming phone call, I can answer it and speak using the built-in microphone.

My watch is synchronized with my headset and my phone so that when I have an incoming call, I can look down and see who it is and decide whether to answer or not. When I am running or cycling I don't want to speak to anyone – in fact, I usually deliberately ignore them because this is *my* time, I am in my Personal Energy Zone and I want to be left alone. This is my opportunity to be at peace with myself and not be disturbed.

Of course, there are exceptions. I may be late, having decided to run or cycle further than originally planned – or I got lost – and my wife is calling to see if I am okay. Someone I have been attempting to speak with for a long time about a very important issue could be calling. But generally, I ignore all calls.

Technology in communication has developed by leaps and bounds over the last century and while this is, of course, a tremendous advantage in many fields and industries, it also has many disadvantages. Imagine you are *Running in the Rain*. It isn't just raining, it is pouring, and lots of big droplets of water are hitting your head, face, and body. It may not feel very comfortable, but as you keep your pace, you start to defeat them, you start to ignore them and eventually, you don't even notice them, because you are determined not to allow a bit of water to keep you from achieving your goal of running whatever distance you had set yourself.

You get home, you peel off your wet clothes, get into a hot shower, and feel great, because you did not allow lots of drops of water to stop you from getting started, to stop you from continuing, or to stop you from finishing.

Now imagine you are working at your desk. Instead of it raining, you are slowly being bombarded with emails, instant messages, and texts. You have several apps open that keep registering notifications and you seem very popular on social media as people keep liking and commenting on your recent posts. But rather than starting to "defeat" them or ignore them because you have to complete a number of important projects from your fairly-full A-List, you react to them. You start reading them and replying. You wait for a response. You start scrolling through other social media platforms; you see a thread, so you start reading it.

What have you done?

You have allowed the rain to win. The rain has defeated you. You have stopped moving forward. You are standing still and soon you will be so far behind in your work you will be effectively going back towards your starting point.

If you were to make a list of all the tools required to be successful in business, as a member of a team or just in life generally, you would almost certainly include the word "communication." The flip side to that is the impact on a person's effectiveness if they are not a good communicator: it makes it tough for them to complete responsibilities in their Professional Energy Zone, as well as in their Personal and Social Zones. In fact, we often think we are strong communicators, when the opposite may be true, and George Bernard Shaw had it right when he uttered the immortal phrase, "The single biggest problem in communication is the illusion it has taken place."

## What Are Your Biggest Challenges?

I have had the fortune of presenting and facilitating hundreds of leadership development workshops during my career and one of the first questions I like to ask participants at any level, from C–Suite executives to junior supervisors, is to define what they feel the biggest challenges they face are in leading or managing their teams. The most common responses are usually related to getting teams to do the job they want them to do and when I ask them to clarify this point, I'm usually met with responses such as:

"I tell my guys what to do, ask them if they have any questions, and tell them to get working, but when I return to check on progress, I see lots of different outcomes – it drives me up the wall."

Of course, CEOs and other senior leadership executives may phrase these types of challenges in a slightly more refined way, but the principle remains the same: their teams are not executing the tasks they are being set, even though they have not asked any questions about them. This results in frustration, rework, a waste of resources, a lack of trust, and probably some significant impact on the customer. The "recipients" of the communication are probably even more frustrated because they want to work on the right tasks in the right way. They don't like having to do their work over. They start to wonder if they were the ones who misheard, or is this manager just bad at communicating with everyone?

As anyone who serves in the military knows, communication is at the root of all activity, and this concept was drilled into me from the first days of my life in uniform. Although I joined the music branch of the Royal Marines, the principles were the same. Indeed, for a unit that was generally performing at high-profile public events, often in front of royalty and Heads of State, plus global television audiences of millions of viewers, they were essential. You need to know where you need to be, what uniform to wear, what equipment you need, what you will be doing, to what level and for how long. You are taught how to listen and take notes and you are offered the chance to ask questions, although you are often vilified if a question is stupid or the answer is obvious, which in turn ensures you listen properly the next time. You are then tested with questions about the details you have been given to ensure you fully understand them.

You then set about executing on your objective.

The principles outlined above are not some draconian process based on regimental tradition, they are proven techniques that ensure everyone knows what to do, and when. They breed trust and confidence and, above all else, they save time, because when orders are issued, there may not be very much time available for execution, so they have to stick at the first attempt.

Clearly understanding your task creates trust, confidence and energy.

This principle outlines my own perspective on communication, although this isn't exclusive to me alone:

> *Communication is only complete when the transmitter has received confirmation back from the receiver that the message is fully understood.*

That confirmation can take many forms, but there needs to be some type of physical and indelible statement.

## Early Days with Blackberry

During my early days in the business world, I was the proud owner of one of the first Blackberry devices, a precursor to the smartphone. Mine was a game-changer for me.

After a day on the road spent meeting with prospects and clients, delivering training and coaching workshops, I would connect my Blackberry to my laptop upon my return to the office, open up the desktop syncing application and watch all the appointments and contacts I had set up during the day flash in front of my eyes as they were transferred from device to device. As each item was transferred, a notification would signal that it had been "synced" so I could tell all was well.

In those pre-wi-fi days, the cable between the two devices effectively functioned as the spoken word between two people and I was only confident I had not missed anything after I had checked both calendars to ensure everything was aligned.

Obsessive, paranoid, over-the-top?

Yes – probably, but I don't ever remember missing an appointment.

As I have grown to trust technology, I don't spend quite so much time cross-checking each device, although I still thoroughly check my schedule on my smartphone *and* laptop at the start of each week. But the Blackberry/laptop synchronization is a fine example of communication:

each device is passing information to the other and getting something back to ensure it is understood.

Fast forward to today and it appears we have almost gone to the extremes in the opposite direction. Our communication is now of demand-a-response type. If we send an email to a colleague and they don't respond within a minute, we walk over to their desk to ask if they got it. We have created many new tools, such as instant messaging, internal chat and Slack, to *improve* communication, but all they really do is slow down productivity by being constantly distracted. We earlier discussed the implications of distractions, and communication is high on the list of causes: the cost and damage of constant interruptions through the barrage of inbound mail is high indeed. So, let's look at some techniques I have been using for many years to not only create relief from the communication burden but also to communicate more efficiently.

## Inbox Discipline

I never realized how poorly disciplined some people are when it comes to their inboxes. I am a tidy person in general – it's part of the genetics I inherited from my parents and my mother instilled in me the principle that "Everything has a place;" she would remind me of this if anything was left lying around the house. I also spent long periods on the ships of the United Kingdom's Royal Navy, learning quickly that I wouldn't last long if I left my kit everywhere: the untidy crewmember received a few warnings, but then his or her belongings were likely to get thrown overboard. I took this principle with me into the world of the internet, particularly my inbox.

Folders are pretty easy to set up and for me, it seemed fairly logical and obvious to create one for each aspect of my professional and personal email accounts. That way, everything is clean and tidy – rather like the front door area of your house: imagine the chaos if everyone who entered just dumped all their stuff on the floor ("But they do!" I hear many of you shout). But while it seemed a simple process to keep my own inbox tidy, over several years of leadership development coaching, I found that it is quite a challenge for many people. I've seen some horrifying numbers of emails in people's inboxes – more than 37,000 in one case – either waiting to be taken care of or saved for later use. Without a search facility, trying to find them could be a week's work on its own.

So, I came up with a process that has apparently changed the lives of many people, and let's start reviewing it by first applying our Goals vs. Routine vs. System principle:

- Goal: To keep my inbox clean and empty so I can manage inbound mail efficiently.

- Routine: To be efficient and responsible when dealing with inbound email, to be able to prioritize emails for action, and to determine which ones to remove.

- System: Develop a simple process for managing inbound email by categorizing all mail and executing with discipline.

## Do Yourself a Good DEED

The word *DEED* reflects accomplishment, action, feat, endeavour, etc. and it's a fitting title for how I treat each and every email that enters my inbox. I class them into one of four categories:

D – Do It

E – Entrust It

E – Erase It

D – Defer It

The first rule to DEED–ing your emails is to start at the top (assuming you are set up to see the latest first). That way you will not be selective or distracted by random emails that take you off the trail of efficiency. By starting with the first email at the top, apply the following principles:

## DO IT:

Read the first email and ask if this will take less than two minutes to action? That is, can I do everything this message requires of me within a short time frame? It may require a simple response – a short paragraph with an update or an acknowledgement, maybe forwarding to another department or colleague or, in fact, no action at all – in which case it should not remain in your inbox, but placed in a relevant folder, or erased.

The DO IT principle means several actions take place. You are completing a task, which means less work later. You are responding to someone who is waiting for you. You are tidying something. Or you are erasing something that adds no value to your life. If you look at an email and do not take action, you simply add more activity to an already busy schedule later. If you know it would only take a moment to deal with it, but you leave it, you have to refocus on the email later, reread it and then do what you could have done now.

The email may look simple and may take less than two minutes to complete, but you may also want to give it some thought, in which case it does not fall into the DO IT category. Being a DO IT person means you are not standing there looking at the rain and debating with yourself whether to run or not. Instead, you are being active, getting out there to get the job done.

## ENTRUST IT:

ENTRUSTING IT means you read the email and consider whether the matter can be entrusted to someone on your team, a subordinate, a colleague, another department, or whatever. I specifically use the word "entrust" because that implies that it is someone else's responsibility to take on this task, and I make a distinction between this concept and the rather more common term, "delegate."

Since my first leadership roles in the military, I have followed a basic principle on delegation, which is that it should be used almost exclusively as an opportunity to develop someone. I have carried this into my business work, and I encourage clients to follow the same path. Delegation is not an opportunity to pass a task the leader or manager doesn't like doing to someone else because they hate doing it. Delegation is an opportunity for someone to grow, to build on their skills and experience and to advance their knowledge and acumen.

Here's what I would describe as the ideal scenario for delegation: Say a sales representative is looking for opportunities for career advancement and as part of his annual review, it is agreed he would benefit from learning more about preparing quarterly department sales reports. While this task is normally the sales manager's responsibility, she invites the sales rep to work on the quarterly sales report as an opportunity for the agreed-upon growth when the finance department requests the departmental reports. The sales rep should not see this as an onerous task, and the sales manager is not simply dumping a job on them.

To entrust a task to someone, by contrast, suggests they are expected to do this work. They are paid to do it, it is part of their responsibilities and they are trained for it. They are also fully compliant in accepting the work as part of their working routine. So, when an email is received, and it clearly relates to a project for whom someone else is responsible, ENTRUST IT, make a note for a follow-up if required and move the email to the appropriate folder.

## ERASE IT:

ERASE IT is the one DEED category that is underused – and probably ignored – more than any other. When I present this option in a class, I see people smile, nod, look up at the sky, then shake their heads and sigh. When I ask them why they reacted in such a way, they tell me they know they need to stop hoarding emails they are not going to do anything with and just get rid of them.

Being a minimalist is easy – being an effective minimalist is not easy. We can all get rid of a property we don't need but are we getting rid of the right property? I have sometimes gone through clothes with the intent of throwing out items I haven't worn in over a year, only to look for that very shirt or jacket a few weeks later. With email, it should really be easier, and yet we still hang on to items in our inbox that we know we are not going to act upon.

There are some simple rules to follow. Ask yourself:

- When did I last work on this project and is it still alive now?
- What benefits do I get from keeping this email?
- Is this email going to benefit my business objectives in any way?
- What is the worst thing that can happen if I ERASE IT?

If we don't ERASE the email, we should apply the other DEED principles to it, rather than allow it to pollute our inbox.

The final step in the ERASE phase is also a simple but generally overlooked action, which is to kill off the source of unnecessary emails. If you are going to ERASE an email, ask yourself if you want to continue to get more like it. The most likely answer will be that you don't. So, take literally a few seconds to scroll down to the *unsubscribe* link and stop them forever.

## DEFER IT:

If the next email you open will take more than two minutes to action, and you cannot ENTRUST it, and you shouldn't ERASE IT, then you should DEFER IT. At this point we draw upon the same principle we discussed in Chapter 3, the ABCs of Focusing Your Time, and we create three folders at the immediate top of our inbox:

- A-List Emails: MUST be done today
- B-List Emails: CAN be done tomorrow or the day after.
- C-List Emails: CAN be done by the end of the week.

If it is not an option to delay opening an email past the end of the day then it should be placed in the A folder.

If it can be actioned tomorrow or the day after, then place it in the B folder.

Anything else should go into the C folder.

A word of caution: the aim of the DEED process is to create an empty inbox, but this does not mean you are bereft of work just because everything looks clean, empty, and very tidy. There needs to be a system in place to ensure you head to your A folder to work on the emails required for that day and to allow you to focus on the less urgent emails as time and importance dictate.

The benefits of this system are very simple: you are in control, you know what to do and when, you are able to ENTRUST mail to those who should be working on it, and you spend less time working your way through a long list of emails looking for what you should be doing.

## Before You Click Send

Following the steps outlined above will allow you to create a simple but efficient process that enables better functionality and flow of work. It will also help focus your energy in accordance with what we discussed in Chapter 4 by reducing the distraction that reacting to emails creates.

So far, I have yet to hear from anyone who has found an email that does not fit into one of the four DEED categories, so everyone who adopts this process has made significant improvements to their workflow.

But what about outbound email – isn't communication a two-way street?

Let's imagine that each time we click "send" on an email, we are physically prodding someone in the arm. I'm not talking about a gentle nudge or a slight tap, I am talking about walking up to them, sticking our index finger out, and ramming it hard into their arm.

Wouldn't that annoy them, wouldn't it just slightly derail their focus from whatever they were doing? And wouldn't they probably either snap back with some form of retaliation or make an effort to get as far away from us as possible and ignore us from that moment onwards? While we are unlikely to go around prodding people in the arm to get their attention, many of us sometimes feel this is what is happening to us when we are bombarded with communication, especially email.

So, what can we do to alleviate the constant traffic we pour into our colleagues' inboxes?

A few years ago, one of my client companies wanted to look into email discipline in order to reduce the amount of internal email traffic and sharpen up best-practice communication. The Senior Leadership Team invited me to a meeting to discuss this topic and during the meeting, my military background prompted the conversation to turn to the subject of submarines. Nuclear submarines are designed to spend very long periods of time underwater, which means they are almost undetectable by satellite no matter where they are in the world.

They still have to communicate, of course, and for many years this meant once a day rising towards the surface of the ocean and despatching a communications beacon attached to a cable that floated upwards and breached the surface of the water. There would then be a 10-second "blast and receive" transmission during which all outbound and inbound communication were sent and received. The beacon would then be lowered, and the submarine submerged to the depths once again, so it remained untraceable by the enemy.

But can you imagine if the submarine captain had to transmit as many signals each day as the average knowledge worker does and for each one he had to get close enough to the surface to be able to float his communications beacon? It would almost certainly mean the submarine might as well surface and wait to be spotted by satellite, reducing the need for the boat in the first place. While the technology on a submarine is pretty advanced, wouldn't it be great if we could complete all our outbound and inbound communications for the day in just 10 seconds, to allow us to plan our day and get on with important tasks and projects?

Well, maybe we can't get it all done in 10 seconds, but we can follow the same principle, which is exactly what we did with my client.

Once I had laid the submarine idea in front of this company's senior leadership team, I got them thinking about the types of emails their teams transmitted each day, and we developed a Goals vs. Routine vs. Systems solution:

- Goal: To reduce the number of internal emails transmitted by 50% within 30 days.

- Routine: To create fewer distractions and a better workflow through better internal communication discipline.

- System: Develop a prioritization category for all internal emails, create *transmit time zones*, train all staff, and assess weekly.

We started by breaking down all internal emails[11] into four categories:

- Critical: The basic rule to this category was to apply the question,

  *If I do not send this NOW, could there be a negative financial impact on the company?*

  If the answer was yes, then the email could be sent at any time and had to be followed up with a text message if the company was in a *Dark Zone* stage.

- Operational: Operational criteria covered business-related communication for which email was the most effective vehicle.

  It included requests from sales reps for confirmation from Operations that a contract could be completed within a certain time frame. Or client feedback from a customer service representative. Operational email responses were not critical, but should be transmitted within two hours and it was important that an electronic audit trail was available.

---

[11] It should be noted that external emails were not included as this was not seen as a distraction to colleagues. However, there were times when external email had to be copied to colleagues, in which case it was up to the recipient to apply the **DEED** principles.

- Routine: For routine communications, we invited a pause while a key question was posed: "Will I be seeing the recipient over the next day – in which case can we discuss it in person?" We then encouraged team members to discuss these types of issues at the beginning of meetings and huddles, although after a period of test and adjust it was agreed that an advance email might be sent to the team to ask them to prepare to discuss their ideas, etc. This made a huge contribution to reducing the *"any thoughts?"* and *"reply all"* traffic that can grind people's workflow to a halt.

- Reference: The final category related to emails that were delivered on a purely FYI basis, but it was instilled in people that they should *not* respond unless absolutely necessary. We encouraged transmitters to include the option for a simple *"opened"* email response, so they knew the information had reached its destination, but no further action was required.

And how did things work out after 30 days?

Well, it took some adjustments and for the first week or so staff were somewhat confused, but once we analyzed the feedback and created some clarification on the precise status of outbound emails, we saw a 25% reduction in the volume of emails within 21 days, which increased to more than 40% by the end of the month.

*Critical* emails had to be thoroughly reviewed, as sometimes people disagreed about what fell into that category. In fact, once people realized that a lot of the email traffic that was traditionally sent was, in fact, not necessary, the volume dropped dramatically.

Achieving our target of a 50% reduction in email volume took another couple of weeks, but once that was in place, firm discipline from the senior leadership team enabled the strategy to become standard operating procedure across all departments.

One interesting outcome was that most staff had earlier felt they had to reply to customer queries almost instantly, when in fact the new system showed the expectation was that responses should generally come within an hour. There were, of course, some exceptions, so staff members who worked on critical accounts would keep their inboxes ready to receive and reply immediately, but generally, the time frame became much more manageable.

My client was a software company and while this technique worked well for them with regard to internal email discipline, it's safe to say this system would be equally compatible in just about every industry.

The challenges we now face with communication relate not so much to the message we want to send, but rather the ease with which we can send it.

While my wonderful headphones do not, thankfully, keep me from *Running in the Rain*, they do offer me the opportunity to filter inbound communications so I can stay in my Personal Energy Zone. But if action is not taken on communication for the average knowledge worker, the constant flow of email, chat, text and other forms of messaging will do nothing but push them into despair. And as we learned from Plato:

> *Wise men speak because they have something to say.*
> *Fools, because they have to say something.*

By controlling what comes in, and thinking carefully about what goes out, we can all be wise men and women.

# CHAPTER 7

# Do You Think You Could Try a Bit Harder?

*No one succeeds without effort... Those who succeed*
*owe their success to perseverance.*

**–Ramana Maharshi**

*I*t was supposed to be ten. I had decided it was going to be ten. My mind was made up, it was going to be ten. Ten it was – or maybe five this week.

I had put Monday mornings aside for a run workout, which was a major change in strategy from just choosing a distance and completing it. I had a big task ahead of me, having qualified to represent Canada in the 2019 World Duathlon Championships in the Sprint category. This is not as short as it may sound as it still involves a five kilometre run and a 20-kilometre bike ride followed by a 2.5 kilometre run. All of which were to be completed *really* fast. And it meant my mind and body had to shift away from long arduous days of running and cycling to shorter and more intense training sessions.

I had thought I had set myself up for an easier year. I mean, anything is easier than seven hours on a bike or four hours of running – right? But the results of the previous year's competitors made it apparent that, if I was going to avoid being embarrassed by some of the fastest duathletes in the world for my age group, I was going to have to learn to run and cycle *a lot* faster than ever before. This meant interval training, where I would run hard for several minutes, then run slowly to recover, and then repeat – several times. And it meant running up hills – repeatedly, a task I saved for Monday mornings so I could get it over with early in the week.

Close to where I lived there was a trail, that while predominantly flat, included a nasty and very steep hill, that even when going full speed took over a minute to ascend. This hill was part of the focus of my Monday mornings and after completing a set of intervals on the flat, I would recover before attempting a set number of hill climbs. I would sprint up as fast as I could, turn around and slowly jog down – then repeat. At first, I would complete five sets, but after a few weeks I began to push the number up to 10 – which was pretty much the limit if I wanted to keep running up the hill, rather than do it at a staggering walk. Then I focused on attempting to beat my time. But on the morning in question things were not looking good.

I had been woken a couple of times in the night by the rain lashing against the window and although it had eased by now, it was still pretty heavy.

My weekend training schedule had been fairly light, with a short bike ride on Saturday and a slow 10 kilometre run on Sunday, so I should have felt quite rested when 5:20 a.m. Monday morning arrived. Except I didn't. Instead, I just wanted to roll over and go back to sleep. As usual, I had set some expectations by laying out my training clothes in the bathroom, so if I didn't train, I had to take the walk of shame and put them back in the closet. And it had been something of a battle of mind over matter just looking at them as I brushed my teeth and listened to the rain on the bathroom window.

"Come back and lie down again," I could hear my bed calling out to me in the back of my mind. But it was Monday, and the week would not start well if I gave in.

"Ten. I am doing 10 hill climbs today," I thought. Once dressed, I downed an espresso to get me going and I was out of the door, into the rain, and jogging down to the trail as part of my warm-up. With stretching done, I went straight into my intervals, which were based on time not distance, so I had no real way of gauging my performance, but I knew I didn't feel up for much that morning. I always finish my intervals about 200 metres from the bottom of the hill so I can take a walk to recover and be ready for the main event, and that morning I knew 10 sets was going to be a real struggle. But off I went. Ten times up and down the hill. In the rain.

## Perceived Effort

Endurance athletes all have one thing in common. They *endure*. They endure long training sessions, long periods of pain, injuries, feelings of thirst and hunger, and often a very restricted lifestyle where many common luxuries are forbidden. However, what endurance athletes have to endure above anything else is not an actual effort, but the *perception of effort*. I'm no scientist, so I like descriptions that are simple and expressed in plain language, which in this case means the question a lot of athletes ask is, "*how hard* is it going to be?"

Having been part of many rugby teams, and having lived a military life, I've heard countless flippant, sarcastic responses to problems and challenges, and these usually made me smile. In most cases, they laid bare the reality of the task ahead. In the context of my hill climb circuit, when I'm feeling tired and not really sure whether I should do 10 reps – a cool word athletes use for *repetitions* – simply say to myself, "I'm going to run up this hill and back 10 times – *how hard can it be?*"

The theory related to the perception of effort is central to the psychobiological model of endurance performance. In other words, if you think it is going to be hard, it will be, even if your body is in pretty good shape to perform. I knew in my mind the morning the rain tested my resolve so badly that those 10 reps were going to be really tough as I wasn't feeling very energetic that day. They were tough even when I felt strong, but on that particular day, 10 reps were just not going to happen. But they did. Perceived effort is really symptomatic of the body arguing with or resisting the mind's intention. To overcome the challenges this condition creates, athletes either have to become fitter – which is never a bad thing, although overtraining can be counterproductive – or they need a coping mechanism to help them overcome and achieve. A powerful mindset around acknowledging the perception of effort is critical for high performance.

Perception of effort relates to how an athlete approaches a challenge. If they perceive the effort to be easy, they will probably underperform. If they think it is going to be tough, they may well increase their effort.

Mo Farrah is one of Great Britain's greatest-ever athletes. He has won multiple Olympic and World Championship Gold medals in the 5,000 – and 10,000 – metre running events. But during a BBC interview prior to his first marathon, he stated it would be his toughest ever race. Farrah was simply acknowledging the headspace he was in and the challenge ahead of him. As it happened, he wasn't too wrong as he still has yet to win a significant marathon. But has Mo Farrah's mindset and approach to the perception of effort negatively impacted his performance? It is worth considering Alan St. Clair Gibson's research report in the British Journal of Sports Medicine following a project in which he studied the performance levels of a number of experienced athletes over set distances.

He started by asking a group of athletes to run for 20 minutes on a treadmill, and after each minute asked them how they felt with regard to enjoyment and perception of effort. He recorded their thoughts and performance levels, such as their heart rate, etc.

He then asked another group of athletes to run at the same pace for 10 minutes and posed the same questions at the same time intervals. But at the end of the 10 minutes, he asked them to continue for another 10 minutes. Testing was carried out in a randomized fashion and no one was permitted to divulge what had happened during the session to their peers.

The data St. Clair Gibson collected revealed that athletes who were told they had to run an extra 10 minutes beyond their initial 10 minute run reported a spike in the perception of effort – and their performance took a nosedive – compared to those who were told from the outset that they had to run for 20 minutes.

Another study reported tests on runners who were timed when sprinting a short distance of 50 metres. They were then asked to sprint the same distance again but were told they might be waved through to do 100 metres in total. Regardless of whether they were waved through or not, they each ran the first 50 metres more slowly than they had when they knew they only had to do 50.

It may seem logical that an athlete will run more cautiously if they think they might have to double the distance they have to run, but this is actually more evidence of the perception of effort, and it plays a very significant part in what we do, how we do it and to what level.

## The Secret to Happiness…

I have been called many things during my life and one of the most common comments I've heard is that I am a *natural pessimist*. I don't take offence to this tag as I find it to be accurate in that I do generally take a less-than-positive approach to tasks that confront me. My theory is that if you expect the worst and you are wrong, then that has to be a nice outcome. Right? I mean, even Homer Simpson might have been on to something when he said, "the secret to happiness is having low expectations." But if you spend your life expecting everything to turn out fine, well, you are probably going to be a bit disappointed along the way. My approach doesn't mean I spend my days in a dark pit of despair expecting the sky to fall and the world to end. But it does mean I feel ready for challenges to be a bit tougher than they may first appear and so I should be well-prepared for whatever comes my way.

Imagine you want to run up a steep hill and you look at it and think it's going to be easy, so you start fast. Halfway up, however, you realize it is much harder than you thought… but you have used up all your energy. Whereas if you look at the hill and think it may well be a bit harder than it appears, you are ready for the point at which the going gets tough.

The same might be applied to baking a rather ornate birthday cake for someone special. No matter how experienced you are at baking, if you think it is going to be – literally – a piece of cake (pun intended), and it turns into something of a less-than-satisfactory culinary extravaganza, the birthday recipient may well feel quite let down by the outcome or the lateness of the final effort. But of course, if you are a student at my school of natural pessimism, you would probably allow longer and take more care over the process, based on the assumption it is going to be more of a challenge than you had at first perceived.

In my military career, I rose to the position of Director of Music, which meant I was ultimately responsible for the quality of the musical output from the musicians under my command. This included the effective scheduling of rehearsals, and my modus operandi was to allocate slightly more time than was probably required to ensure we were not rushed, or the quality negatively impacted. If we got through the rehearsal ahead of schedule, then that meant some downtime for the musicians, which was good for morale. I believed this was better than having to extend rehearsals because of poor planning.

But how does the perception of effort relate to concepts like Energy Zones and productivity?

The key is to assume tasks are going to be at least a little bit harder than you might first think. In a business context, a project may appear to be a routine process that has been completed several times in the past, in which case many members of the team might feel it will not require too much effort. This takes any feelings of urgency out of the equation, leading to mistakes and potential failure.

## 10 x 10 x 10

One of the more basic mistakes an inexperienced athlete makes is to start too fast, then either fail to finish or simply run out of energy. This is almost the reverse idea of the perception of effort, as though the athlete is saying, "this is easy, watch me go!"

There is a simple strategy that when effectively applied, can speed up an overall time.

Take a marathon, which is run over a 26-mile and 385-yard distance. This can also be envisioned as a distance of approximately 20 miles plus 10 kilometres.

The 10 x 10 x 10 strategy requires you to set yourself a time, then calculate the average pace you will need to maintain for the full distance. You then break the race into three sections: the first 10 miles, the second 10 miles, and the last 10 kilometres.

Your plan is then to run the first 10 miles slightly slower than your overall pace, so at the end of that section, you may be down on your target time, but you will not be tired and you will therefore be ready to increase your pace at a time when you would normally start to reduce it due to fatigue.

For the second 10 miles, you run at a slightly faster pace than your overall average, which will make up for the lost time and push you to the last leg of the marathon.

Then, for the final six miles (or 10 kilometres) you pour every drop of energy you have into a big last effort.

For most runners using this strategy, the hardest part is to run the first 10 miles at a slower pace than they are used to because their perception of the effort they are making will put them well behind on the clock. But if they fail to stay at a slow pace, then they are unlikely to achieve their target time due to early fatigue.

## Don't Work Forwards – Work Back

In the context of our workday it is, of course, a basic fact that we work forward towards an objective because unless one is a character in a science fiction story, it is not possible to travel back in time. But the most successful strategists among us will often plan backward from the objective to the starting point and thereby create a logical outline of what needs to be done, to what level, and by when.

Perception of effort plays a part in this process, as well, because by laying out the course in reverse order, the key points of when we will be working the hardest can be easily identified. Take the 10 x 10 x 10 principle discussed above. You know that to achieve a good finish time you are going to have to give everything you have left in the last 10 kilometres of the marathon.

But in order to achieve a fast time in the last 10 kilometres, you have to maintain an above-average pace during the second 10 miles of the race.

And to allow yourself to conserve energy for the second 10 miles as well as the final 10 kilometres, you need to run at a below-average pace for the first 10 miles.

We just built a strategic mindset working *back* from the finish, which will help us understand the importance of saving ourselves during the first 10 miles, which is quite different from starting the race and not truly appreciating the importance of a slow early pace.

There are a number of key principles involved in implementing a work–back schedule:

1. Choose a non-negotiable deadline.
2. Create landmarks between project completion and start time.
3. Define the very first step with a specific objective and deadline.

## The Non–Negotiable Deadline

The completion date for a task must be clearly defined and wherever possible it must be indelible. If those executing the task know there will be opportunities to move the deadline back, then focus will be lost and excuses will be made. This will result in a lack of effort and a generally less-than-efficient outcome. No matter the perception of effort required to complete the task, if there are movable outcomes, then we simply concede to the *feeling* the idea of too much effort generates and we fail to optimize the opportunity for good work.

When I set out on my weekly hill climb set, I want the concept of 10 reps to be indelibly etched in my mind so that it becomes a non-negotiable target.

Likewise, with business objectives, the completion date for a project must be non-negotiable. Otherwise, if team members believe it can be moved, they will not be as focused or motivated as necessary in order to achieve the objective in a timely fashion: it is natural to perceive the amount of effort required as less than they had initially assumed because they now have more time available and there is less pressure on them to get moving. Quality is often the victim.

## Create Landmarks

While we generally create landmarks for our projects subconsciously, I am never surprised when I meet people who seem to struggle with this concept, so formalizing the process can often be very helpful.

As mentioned earlier, rather than starting by looking at checkpoints moving forward from the present to completion, it is better to move back from completion, through specific landmarks, to our start point. The dates of the landmarks are fairly simple to define (where do we need to be one month out, two months out, and three months out?). But the key to putting these markers in place are the sub-objectives that need to be complete by these points in time. Defining criteria for what we should complete by when gives us a better perception of the effort required and it means the project will proceed as planned so we can achieve our overall objective.

## Define First Steps

Often the first steps are the hardest, but once we have things moving then we are able to proceed towards our first landmark... as long as we maintain momentum. I have been in many planning sessions with clients who have spent long hours laying out their strategy for a project with supposedly clear objectives and defined tasks. As they wrap things up, confidently believing everything is in place for the completion of a successful project, I like to ask the question, "what is your very first task and when does it need to be completed?"

The common response is either dead silence or a heated debate about what should indeed happen first. This simply shows me that unless this question is answered, the first landmark is unlikely to be achieved to the required level, or even on time, and this will probably put the project back and require a change in the now clearly negotiable deadline.

## Application

Let's take this discussion into the approach I like to adopt for an Ironman race. In the Town of Mont Tremblant, Quebec, an Ironman Triathlon is traditionally held on the third Sunday of August. More than 2,500 athletes, from professionals to "age groupers," compete in this gruelling event and unless there is a delay for the weather – sometimes caused by fog on the lake, which makes a long open water swim unsafe – the start cannon sounds at 6:30 a.m. If ever you want an example of a non-negotiable deadline, this is it, because if an athlete does not feel ready to start the race due to an injury or lack of training, no matter how hard they try, they are not going to convince the race organizers and all the other competitors that the start time should be delayed by a few weeks. That cannon is fired on time – whether you are ready or not.

Landmarks for an Ironman are fairly simple. Around three weeks before race day you enter "peak week." This means you put yourself through some intense distances in order to push your body prior to tapering down on distance and effort in the two weeks or so leading up to the race. The goal is to greet the day of the competition feeling well-trained and rested.

Around two months out, I like to be comfortable with travelling at least half the full distance required by the competition, and I often complete a half Ironman race in preparation. And at three months from race day, I will be increasing distances to at least one-third of the final total, as well as completing some Olympic and sprint distance races.

Defining the first steps for an Ironman race are more logistical than physical in that this stage includes completing my race entry and booking my accommodation, without which my involvement in the race is not going to happen. And I like to secure these components at least 11 months out.

The benefits of a work-back schedule are many-faceted, but for me, they are a critical aspect of assessing the effort required to complete a task and make a valuable contribution to ensuring deadlines are not missed. Furthermore, work is well planned without the need for last-minute panicking, which often leads to burnout and poor performance.

## The Nike Paradox

In 1996, the American sportswear manufacturer, Nike, produced a video featuring arguably the greatest basketball player in history, Michael Jordan, to promote their brand of shoes, the Jordan XIs. This commercial was part of a long series of commercials in support of Jordan-branded products. It was also part of their *Just Do It* campaign, which along with the famous Nike *swish* motif, is an excellent example of successful branding, making this company one of the largest players in their industry. The *Just Do It* campaign was launched in 1988 and featured amateur and professional athletes talking about their accomplishments and the emotions they felt as they exercised. In the 1996 video, Jordan is seen walking into a very large and empty arena with a basketball net at one end, but rather than being fitted to a traditional stand, the net is on a long pole and appears to be around 100 feet in the air.

Jordan bounces the ball a few times as the camera focuses on his white Jordan XI shoes, then pans back to see him run across the floor before taking a huge leap, after which he flies through the air, dunks the ball, and grabs the rim of the basket. As he hangs in mid-air, he stares at the camera with a look of surprise on his face over the fact he has leaped so high and is stuck 100 feet off the ground. The words *Just Do It* then appear on the screen followed by an image of the shoes the commercial is designed to promote. The campaign embodied Nike's image as an innovative and iconic American company associated with success. The combination of professional athletes and motivational slogans emphasizing sportsmanship and health led to customers associating their purchases with the prospect of achieving greatness and the message (as per all great marketing content) was very simple: don't think about it – *Just Do It*, especially if you have the best equipment money can buy.

This commercial resonated with me at a critical time in my military career as 1996 was the year I was chosen to attend officer selection, the process through which potential Royal Marines officers are assessed and selected. This was a particularly challenging experience that would define much of the remainder of my career and life. As well as working on in-depth academic courses, I was also determined to increase my fitness levels to new heights, which involved a lot of training and hard work. I had never really paid a lot of attention to sports commercials or their branding messages. At least, not consciously – although any decent marketing guru would probably tell me I was subconsciously "buying-in." But this ad got my attention. I resonated with the image of someone looking at a ridiculously high basketball net, not even thinking about the impossibility of the task ahead, but instead just running and jumping as high as he could. And if he got stuck 100 feet off the ground... well, he'll worry about that later. I don't think I even knew who Michael Jordan was at the time, but in line with the concept behind *Running in the Rain*, he just got on with it.

The task ahead of me during my preparation for officer selection was harder than anything I had done in my career, and while I worked hard, the natural pessimist in me was preparing for failure. As usual. In the past, both in my career and as a sportsman, most of my challenges and accomplishments had been completed as part of a team, where the *esprit de corps* had played a part in the environment leading towards either the group's success or its failure. But now I was on my own. There was no one else to depend on and my mindset would mean everything if I were to be successful in gaining a commission as a Royal Marines officer.

Mindset. Perception of Effort. How hard could it be? These concepts all combined to play tricks on me, but thanks to Nike, the basic premise of *Just Do It* came through loud and clear and I became committed to my preparatory work and my physical fitness, resulting in successful selection for a commission. The rest, you might think, is history.

Well, not quite.

As with their relationship with Michael Jordan, Nike has large sponsorship deals with many other athletes, including the American sprinter Justin Gatlin. Gatlin tested positive for amphetamines in 2001 and was banned from competition for two years, which was reduced on appeal. On his reinstatement to the sport, Nike continued their sponsorship, paying Gatlin millions of dollars. Then in 2006, he tested positive again, this time for testosterone, and he was awarded an eight-year ban. He avoided a lifetime ban only because he cooperated with the authorities over other performance-enhancing practices of which he was aware. He then appealed again, and the ban was reduced to four years.

Gatlin returned to athletics in 2010, a twice-convicted cheat, and went on to win the 100 metre Gold Medal at the World Championship in Doha, Qatar, in 2017. Although Nike had dropped him in 2006 after his second conviction, they renewed his contract in 2015 and went on to build their relationship with him, continuing to sponsor him to the tune of millions of dollars. The paradox for me in all this lies with the issue that a brand that so inspired me in 1996 then went on to destroy everything about integrity and fair play that I believed in. Since 2015 I have refused to buy or wear the Nike brand because the *Just Do It* message is now a tarnished and hollow shell. Indeed, it is now applied to a cheat, because when Justin Gatlin was considering injecting himself with a performance-enhancing substance, he didn't seem to think too much about it – he just went ahead and did it. Or as Nike might say *Just Do It* Justin – we're okay with cheating.

Did quitting on a brand take much effort on my part? It shouldn't have but, actually, it did. I liked the Nike products and was often given them as gifts, but I had to tell my family and friends that I could not accept them in principle. I refused to go into Nike stores, or even use their golf balls when they were handed out as part of a package at charity golf events. But the effort it took to do this was not really of a physical or practical nature. Instead, it related to the mindset I decided to adopt towards this brand. In this case, the perception of effort was quite simple: I felt it was morally inappropriate to continue to support this brand by buying their products. And once that was firmly ingrained in my principles, I was able to move on quite effortlessly.

How much effort does it take to *run in the rain*? Thinking about it logically, it is not much different from running in the dry, except you get wet, and unless you are going a very long distance with wet shoes and socks, it really isn't much of an inconvenience. So why do we make so much of an issue out of it – avoid it – make excuses – delay the start – in the hope the weather will dry up? I believe the answer is that we perceive that *Running in the Rain* is going to be a very unpleasant experience when actually it really isn't. So we should ideally just stop messing around and get on with it.

I mean – seriously, *how hard can it be?*

# CHAPTER 8

# What Are You Waiting For?

*You may delay, but time will not, and lost time*
*is never found again.*

**–Benjamin Franklin**

*I* opened the weather app on my phone, and although I knew it was raining outside, wanted to check the forecast for the next few days. Rain today, rain tomorrow, and rain the day after. I was in the city of Seattle on the US northwest coast for a three-day conference. The Emerald City, named after its plentiful acreages of lush green plants and trees, would not merit the nickname without an abundant supply of rainfall. I had been warned, and they were wise words. Coming to Seattle? Bring your raincoat or, in this case, your running rain jacket.

I have a simple objective when travelling on business or for pleasure: wherever I go I like to run. This has resulted in some wonderful experiences in some of the most famous – and not so famous – locations in the world, and in some of the most extreme weather conditions. From the energy-sapping humidity of places like Bangkok and Singapore to the dry heat of the Egyptian desert to the high altitude and thin air of Bogota and Mexico City, to the freezing cold of Sevastopol – where your own personal icicles cause your eyelids to freeze shut. I have run in more than 50 countries and in pretty much every weather condition.

But today it was Seattle and rain. Rain today. Rain tomorrow. And rain the day after.

If you want to find an event that justifies procrastination, look no further than when you are planning on going for a run and rain is lashing down. You look outside and wonder if it is going to stop and no matter what the forecast says, you probably hope there will be a break in the near future. You consider your clothing options: rain jacket that might make you too hot. Or, if it is warm, you might just go in a shirt and get soaked. Shoes? Probably not your new pair, so that old pair that have very little life left in them will do for wet weather and short runs. And socks or no socks? Wet socks are not pleasant, but bare feet in wet shoes? Hmmm. Visor or cap? Probably the cap so it keeps the rain off your head. And what about headphones? Those new Apple earbuds were ridiculously expensive and probably aren't waterproof. And you'll need a waterproof bag for your phone.

Once the running kit is decided, another weather check appears logical. Still raining. Maybe another espresso.

Did I turn the bathroom light off? Better check.

Is the backdoor locked? Better check.

Maybe I will wear socks after all as these shoes feel a bit loose.

And gloves? Where did I put them?

Right then – ready to go. But look at the time. It looks like this will have to be a quick run around the block and back – or maybe I should try again later in the day when it has brightened up a bit?

I once heard procrastination described as *The Disease of the Intelligent*. The more you know about something, especially the negative aspects of it, the longer it will take you to get started on it. We'll expand on this a little later, but since this is a challenge that most of us face at some point in our lives, if not in our daily activities, it is worth looking into some background, and especially the medical reasoning behind it.

On a neurological level, there is not much about procrastination that is, indeed, logical. The cause is usually the result of the emotional part of the brain, the limbic system, taking over the reasonable, rational part, which is called the prefrontal cortex. The emotional part of your brain gives at the moment you choose an alternative to a task you know you are supposed to be doing. In his book, *Solving the Procrastination Puzzle*, Tim Pychyl identifies a number of triggers that make us more averse to completing tasks, and we are probably all aware that it doesn't usually take much for us to find something a lot more appealing to be doing – even if it is nothing – than the task we have been putting off for some time. The task we are avoiding might be boring, frustrating, quite hard, unclear, or not well planned. It might involve a lot of detailed work, offer little reward or have no personal meaning. Or it could be outright frightening and dangerous. Hold that thought for a while.

There are innumerable books and articles written on this subject, as well as an entire series of podcasts dedicated to solving this eternal struggle. I have spoken to educational course designers who have spent hundreds of hours creating programs to help fix procrastination, but their students either didn't turn up to start the program or, if they did, they failed to get around to completing it. No kidding.

There are probably more famous quotes for procrastination than any other topic, and every notable management expert has their own cure, or at least they think they do. And yet it is hard to find anyone who claims to be free from this condition while always managing to get tasks done without hesitation or delay.

## The Problem of Intelligence

*The Disease of the Intelligent.* I know I heard that phrase somewhere and I can't remember where, or who said it, but it got me thinking because

I believe the originator of the statement had a good point. The phrase also led me to a personal experience I plan never to repeat. Let me start by declaring I have a lifelong fear of heights, although I have been informed several times by wise sages that it is not the height of which I am afraid, rather it is the falling. Throughout my military career I never quite grasped why anyone would want to be a parachutist – I mean, why would any sensible person jump out of a perfectly serviceable aircraft that is quite capable of landing them on the ground while they remain in their seat? I prefer to keep my feet firmly on the ground.

And it is that logical train of thought that I took with me to my first (and last) experience of bungee jumping. My wife planned a family vacation to Vancouver Island to visit her sister and family a few years ago and as part of the few days we were there, some excursions were proposed, one of which was to a tree-walking centre, which also offered bungee jumping. My stepdaughters, who at the time were aged 18 and 15, decided they were going to give it a go. And I was expected to join them. Being a responsible step-parent I decided it might not be in good form to display fear or weakness, so despite a few weeks of trepidation, went along with the adventure and was pleasantly surprised to see the bridge we would be descending from wasn't too high at all. It was still far enough to kill you if the rope was too long or not tied on at the other end, but the fall did not include the spine-chilling distance I had imagined.

Then, as we got closer, I saw we were standing at the top of a ravine and the total distance from the platform to a very rocky riverbed was around 10 times further than I had at first assumed. We were first up after lunch and as there was no lineup, we headed up the steps and along the bridge to the launch point. This was around the time that I realized procrastination was *NOT* going to be a good strategy: I wanted to get off that bridge as quickly as possible. Delaying was only going to make matters worse, so I made it clear I was going first: "let me at it!" I thought. The young "flight attendant" smiled and told me to stand still as he fastened the end of the long elastic rope around my lower legs. He asked me if it felt comfortable, then opened a little gate and told me to jump whenever I was ready.

I knew from my experience as a kid jumping and diving from boards in the swimming pool that waiting wasn't a good idea. Any delay would be met by the abuse and amusement of my mates. So I let my basic strategy take over, shuffled forward, and hurled myself off. The video taken by my wife is actually quite respectable and I made a half-decent attempt at a swallow dive before bouncing up and down for a few minutes before being lowered into a small rubber boat for recovery. I was really quite proud of myself and later that evening over a few drinks, made light of the fact it was no big deal, it was just a bungee jump – whatever. But in hindsight, my mind played back what had happened, and what *could have* happened.

We had to sign a disclaimer, of course, so that if I had gone hurtling into the riverbed at an ever-increasing rate of knots, we couldn't sue the tour company. But as we hear examples of adventure activities going wrong every now and then, I considered how I might have taken a more logical approach to the events of that afternoon.

*The Disease of the Intelligent.* Prior to attaching myself to an elastic rope and throwing myself off a 200-foot bridge, there were a few questions that probably needed to be answered. Rather than trusting in the equipment and the staff, hoping for the best, and just jumping, I might have enquired as to the safety record of the operators. How much training had the guy who tied the rope to my legs gone through? What was his success rate at doing his job right? *Probably* 100%, but that was not guaranteed, right? There were many options for ropes. Was this the right one? Was it short enough? After all, too short is better than too long for this sort of thing.

On balance, trusting in those responsible and jumping was better than hanging around to ask questions, delaying, and making the eventual jump even more of an issue. And therein lies one of the main reasons why we procrastinate: we overthink things, we may be aware of the amount of work involved, and we hesitate. Too much knowledge can be a dangerous thing, so don't think about it too much – just jump.

## Just Get The Truck Moving

You may have seen a program on television or through a streaming service entitled *The World's Strongest Man*. It involves a bunch of extraordinarily strong men competing against each other in a variety of challenges, all of which are designed to test their levels of strength. They must hold huge logs of wood over their heads. Carry concrete boulders across a set distance. Load barrels onto a shelf and complete other weight-based challenges. While strength is at the heart of the various tests, there is also a certain amount of technique involved, especially in the "truck-pull" round, where each competitor is attached to a harness and a rope; this is in turn attached to a very large 18-wheel truck, which they have to pull for 22 metres. These trucks weigh around 50,000 pounds (22,680 kilograms), so getting them moving is quite an achievement, even if it does not appear they have far to travel. The interesting part is that once the competitors get the truck moving, completing the task is relatively smooth sailing as long as they don't ease off on their effort. In fact, in many cases the further they travel the faster they go.

This draws many comparisons with procrastination. Often the hardest part is getting things moving and, once you do, the trick is to not ease off. In fact, pretty much everyone I have advised on this subject has found that once they get started, they want to keep moving and usually complete the task they have been holding off on at a faster rate than they originally thought possible.

And so, I've come up with a simple system that both merges some traditional procrastination tools with a few key points for added effectiveness.

## The Procrasti-Cutioner

The objective of the *Procrasti–Cutioner* is to kill off procrastination (I know, the title isn't the greatest, but as I have been using it for a while now, I'm kind of stuck with it).

As with everything else, let us apply our *Goals vs. Routine vs. System* theory to this tool:

- Goal: I want to stop procrastinating.
- Routine: I want to be more efficient at getting the unpopular tasks done, to free me up to do the things I enjoy.
- System: Adopt the *Procrasti–Cutioner* to the tasks over which I procrastinate.

How do you eat an elephant? One bite at a time – right?

This age-old piece of advice may not be of help to everyone, but the principle of it makes a good point. Very large tasks are unlikely to get completed if you don't break them down into smaller pieces, but having a system to achieve this will help.

There are a number of steps involved – and they need to be followed.

Step 1: Define the actual task you want to complete. Don't generalize, be specific, and set a non-negotiable completion date.[12]

Step 2: Take the task and break off three or four chunks and write them down. The chunks do not need to cover the whole task in its entirety. They do not need to be too specific – just break off large components of what needs to be done and note them down.

Step 3: Take the chunks and divide them into halves. Write down a heading for each half as if it were a simple task that you can complete within a few hours.

Step 4: Take one of the halves and assess how long it will take to complete. If you estimate the time to be longer than two

---

[12] See Chapter 6 for Work-Back Schedules.

hours, it is too large a task and should be divided again. All the tasks you now have in front of you should have a maximum estimated completion time of no longer than two hours.

Step 5: Take one of those sub-tasks and divide the time you estimate it will take by two, so you now have something you need to do that will take no longer than an hour to complete.

Step 6: Add this task (which will take no longer than an hour to complete) to your ABC List and complete it as you would any other task.

You now have the truck moving, so it is important not to ease off. The sub-task was originally estimated as a two-hour commitment before it was divided in half. If you did not complete it in the hour you allocated, simply add another hour to your ABC List and keep going.

If you completed the task within the hour allocated, go back to your original list and select another sub-task. Divide it in half and allocate it to your ABC List, and so on.

If you completed what you originally thought was a two-hour task in less than the hour – and many people do – either fill the hour up with another task or take the time to revise your *Procrasti–Cutioner* chart, make any necessary adjustments, and keep the truck moving.

This may all sound pretty technical and a bit heavy, but when you break it down, it is fairly simple. Imagine you bought a new house about five years ago and have been meaning to finish your basement. Your kids are coming to the age when they no longer want to watch TV with you, so you need to build a separate area, or you just want somewhere to spread out or whatever… in any case, you are long overdue to get the basement finished.

By applying the *Procrasti–Cutioner* to this project, things may look like this:

Step 1: Define the actual task you want to complete and set a non-negotiable completion date.

Complete a full basement renovation by the end of three months.

Step 2: Take the task and break off three or four chunks and write them down.

| Define Budget | Find Contractor | Assess Proposals | Complete Work |
|---|---|---|---|

There are of course many other components to finishing a basement, but remember, all we are doing here is getting the truck moving.

Step 3: Take each chunk and divide it into two halves. Write down a heading for each half as if it is a simple task that you can complete within a few hours.

- Define Budget: How much cash do we have available and how much might we have to borrow?
- Find Contractor: We can search the internet and also ask some neighbours who have recently done similar work.
- Assess Proposals: We may decide to secure three estimates, then choose the most appropriate and sign off.
- Complete the Work: Once we have agreed on the project costs and design, the work has to get started and the completion managed.

Basement Renovation

| Define Budget | | Find Contractor | | Assess Proposals | | Complete Work | |
|---|---|---|---|---|---|---|---|
| Available Capital | Loan Costs | Search Web | Talk to Neighbours | Secure and Read Three Proposals | Decide, Agree and Sign | Agree on Start Date | Oversee Completion |

Step 4: Take one of the halves, create a specific task, and assess how long it will take to complete. If you estimate the

time to be longer than two hours, it is too large a task and should be divided again. All the tasks you now have in front of you should have a maximum estimated completion time of no longer than two hours.

| Available Capital | Loan Costs | Search Web | Talk to Neighbours | Secure and read 3 | Decide, agree & sign | Agree Start Date | Oversee Completion |
|---|---|---|---|---|---|---|---|
| | | | | | | | |

| Specific Task | Estimated Time |
|---|---|
| Search the Web for potential contractors to complete basement project. Look for at least three. | Two Hours |

Step 5: Take one of those sub-tasks and divide the time you estimate it will take by two, so you now have something you need to do that will take no longer than an hour to complete.

| Task | Time Allocation |
|---|---|
| Search the web for three contractors | 1 Hour |

Step 6: Add this task (which will take no longer than an hour to complete) to your ABC List and complete it as you would any other task.

| Task | Time Allocation |
|---|---|
| Search the web for three contractors | 1 Hour |

| A | B | C |
|---|---|---|
| | | |

If you have not found three potential contractors within the allocated hour, simply return the task to your ABC List for the next day. If you accomplished your objective within the hour, apply the same principle to the next task and, if you complete that task before the hour's up, fill the time with the next task, or the planning thereof.

If procrastination is an issue you find difficult to overcome, having a system can be a great help. For many people, it really is just about getting the truck moving and once they are into the sub-tasks outlined above, they are often surprised by the amount of work they can do on a project, which in turn makes them feel better about themselves.

## Team Procrastination

It often only takes one person with the right intent and inspiration to get a team moving in the right direction, but unfortunately, not every team has that person. Indeed, there are certainly leaders around who subconsciously create and develop procrastination without knowing it. As someone who likes to get on with projects rather than hanging around and delaying, I had a really bad experience several years ago when I reported to a manager who was a quintessentially analytical person. Never had the phrase *paralysis through analysis* been more appropriate than when applied to this guy. Meetings would last for hours. He would regularly work 14 hour days and he was surprised when his team didn't appear to want to do likewise. And yet his productivity was terrible. As a team, we were constantly embarrassed about the quality of the work we produced because even though our boss thought we needed to plan, plan and plan again, this didn't make us perform any better or produce anything other than average results. And certainly, projects were not always completed on time.

Thankfully, I had the opportunity to move on and to this day am not sure how I would have ended up if I had to spend another few weeks working for him. I went on to work for some fine, dynamic and inspirational leaders who taught me many skills.

A phrase that has always stuck with me is, "a wrong decision is better than no decision." If you are not sure what to do next, just do something. And this is where a system like the *Procrasti–Cutioner* works for teams as well as individuals.

When applying this process, the benefits arise when the first tasks are allocated to a team, and they then break them down into sub-tasks. Again, it is all about getting the truck moving. You can steer it later, but first, you have to get it going forward.

## Productive Procrastination

Only a fool would claim they have created a guaranteed cure for procrastination, and although many people have told me my system works for them, there will still be occasions when even a simple sub-task is just not going to happen during the time set aside for it. Taking a break and acknowledging a task will have to wait for another day can be refreshing, as long as you know you *will* get to it. To sweeten the mental anguish of not getting that task done, the act of "productive procrastination" can be a good backup plan.

What is that? It is simply filling in the time available with lots of simple and easy tasks that will need to be done at some point, so now is as good a time as any. This is a fine opportunity to *Tap the Bucket*.[13]

## Time To Get Wet

If you are in Seattle, Washington and the weather station forecasts three days of solid rain, you can probably take it as accurate. What's the point in procrastinating on your daily run? It won't change the weather and even though the hotel fitness suite has a few treadmills, to be honest, I would rather get wet.

---

[13] See Chapter 3 for more on "Tapping the Bucket."

# CHAPTER 9

# So You Think YOU Have Had It Hard?

*It is your reaction to adversity, not the adversity itself, that determines how your life's story will develop.*

**–Dieter F. Uchtdorf**

ave you ever had a morning when you get the feeling the day ahead is not going to work out too well? It could be due to a bad night's sleep. Or you might be feeling pretty rough. Maybe your alarm didn't sound, which makes you late. You break your fried eggs before they are cooked. Your car won't start. You want to go for a run but it's raining.

Adversity is a noun that has been part of the English language for more than 800 years. It comes from the Latin *ad versus*, which is literally defined as "turned against," and figuratively defined as "hostile or unfavourable." It is often used slightly mistakenly in place of "mischance," which is really a minor inconvenience rather than a serious or critical situation. It can be pretty obvious when someone has placed themselves into a bad situation due to their own stupidity or lack of understanding, but most often we find ourselves in an adverse situation through no fault of our own. And we all react in different ways when that happens. Let's take a look at the six main categories of adversity because for many people, *Running in the Rain*, is a form of adversity on its own – so let's put things in perspective.

## Physical Adversity

The most obvious example of physical adversity is some form of physical disability which has either been present since birth or acquired through an accident or a sports injury, and which has left the individual in a wheelchair or suffering from the loss of a limb or one of their senses. Other less drastic but similarly problematic types of physical adversity include chronic pain, fatigue, obesity and eating disorders, and although some issues may appear insignificant, it is the afflicted who are ultimately best able to judge their severity. The spectrum of possibilities here is vast.

And are all these "facts of life" or are some sufferers culpable in the creation of their own misfortune? A smoker may claim to be dealing with adversity if he or she contracts lung cancer, but observers may feel they have clearly made a contribution to their condition after many years of nicotine addiction.

Is someone who was born with a limb missing facing more adversity than a soldier whose chosen career took him on operations during which he was severely injured?

And is a brilliant Olympic gymnast who falls and suffers an irreparable ankle injury that ends her career facing more adversity than a young girl who has suffered from rheumatoid arthritis from the age of six?

As I got older and my rugby career started to develop, I began playing in ever more demanding leagues, which basically meant the guys I was up against were getting much bigger and much faster.

This also meant the morning after every game got increasingly more painful. Rugby is played with no protective equipment and it requires strong, fast, athletic and often very heavy players to launch themselves at each other with the objective of stopping or passing their opponent through sheer physical strength or speed. It is not uncommon for ten 200-pound men to pile on top of each other numerous times during a game, crushing the poor person trapped at the bottom of the pile with literally a ton of weight. It's a game played with a distinctly assertive and competitive flair and, after it's all over, and a winner has been declared, members of both teams traditionally repair to the clubhouse bar to relive the game in a spirit of collegial fraternity. Alas, while anyone who has played rugby and is wise to the joys of the game will understand, any non-combatants in my life would simply shake their heads and wonder why I did these things to myself.

Were the feelings of physical adversity I felt I faced after each game justified or was the adversity self-inflicted and purely of my own making, and therefore unworthy of compassion?

As a rugby player, it always seemed a matter of pride that we "played on" no matter how hard we had been hit or how much we were hurting. The game is safer now with head injury assessments at youth and professional levels, but a few years ago we really just got on with it. As a rugby player, I contrast that with American football where players are trussed up in all sorts of padding and helmets, and each team seems to have a hundred or more players – I know, I'm exaggerating here – with the ball barely in play for more than 10 minutes each game. From my perspective, the level of physical adversity evident in American football is nowhere near as arduous as it is in rugby. And yes, I know, I'm a rugby player.

And then there is good old soccer, with its millionaire prima donnas rolling around like they have been shot by a sniper every time they get tackled.

Physical adversity?

I'm not convinced.

I was lucky to survive a 26-year military career relatively unscathed, but many of my colleagues did not, earning mental and physical challenges that left them facing adversity in many and varied forms. We will refer to mental adversity shortly, but for a very fit and active young person to lose three limbs in their early twenties is probably amongst the most extreme forms of physical adversity out there, and you only have to look at events such as the Invictus Games to witness these courageous people working to heroic levels to overcome their situation.

Significant physical adversity doesn't just come from huge bodily dysfunctions and some readers may call me a bit wussy for bringing the following conditions to light. But, if you have suffered either of them, you may well empathize:

**Ingrown Toenails.** Ever had one? If you have, you'll know those things can ruin your whole day, week, or month. I had a history of them as a teenager and although I had surgery to remove the roots in my right big toe before I took the Queen's shilling,[14] the surgeon didn't have a good day and it grew back, albeit it at around only half its original thickness. It was still large enough to bury itself back inside my big toe. In fact, that toenail indirectly gave me a concussion on one occasion. Here's what happened: after battling with it for several months, I ended up on the table in a military sick-bay with a very enthusiastic Royal Navy Chief Petty Officer determined to end its life on account of the fact that he also ran the unit rugby team and needed me to play fly-half the following Saturday.

As I lay down he told me to leave my left boot on and to keep that leg off the table while he anesthetized the guilty toe and cut out the responsible nail. The procedure took around 30 minutes, which was just about enough time to completely cut off the blood supply to my left leg, which had been weighed down by a large combat boot and hanging at a weird angle. Once done, the Chief told me to get up, but to avoid putting any weight on my right foot, at which point I rolled off the table and tried to stand on my left leg. Now completely numb, it immediately

---

[14] "Taking the Queen's Shilling" is an old traditional phrase meaning "to join the British Military."

gave way, sending me straight to the floor, whereupon I hit my head and knocked myself out.

A few years later, the nail was back to its old tricks and while waiting for yet another removal procedure I was asked to referee a services rugby game in the absence of the appointed referee who had got lost getting to the game. Or something. There was no way I was playing with a septic toe that had grown to around twice its normal size, so, borrowing a very large pair of boots, I was happy to oblige and actually managed to keep my toe out of harm's way until partway through the second half, when a particularly large prop forward – one of the biggest players on the field – trod on it.

Now that *really* hurt.

Another by-product of living with an ingrown toenail is the array of counteractions your body takes to compensate for the pain and discomfort. Running requires you to turn your foot to a slightly different angle so your toe doesn't hurt. This then takes your knee out of its traditional alignment, which then screws up your hip, which is passed on to your lower back. It was no coincidence that sciatica was the bane of my life until I finally got my toenail travails fixed, courtesy of a Royal Air Force surgeon. (No, the Chief Petty Officer didn't get all the root out either.) By now you are probably shaking your head in pity that we are using ingrown toenails as examples of adversity.

Okay, then, let's go one step further.

One evening in April 2012, while doing some work in sports sponsorship, I attended a corporate banquet in Hamilton, Ontario, and have to say I enjoyed an excellent meal of steak, followed by a rather exquisite chocolate torte covered in a raspberry drizzle. One of the advantages of attending this event was that I was able to sit with a group of professional ice hockey players who were about to head into their league playoffs, and they were being extremely careful about their diets, as were their wives and girlfriends. I, however, was *not* being too careful about my diet and gratefully received several of their desserts, which left me feeling happy, but really not too comfortable.

On waking up the following morning, I thought I was still feeling the effects of said dessert overdose and hoped the pain I was experiencing – mostly in my lower abdomen but slowly spreading throughout my body – would recede while taking the dog for his first walk of the day.

It didn't.

In fact, the pain got worse, until it was so severe I collapsed on my bathroom floor unable to move. As the rest of the family had gone to their various places of work or learning, the house was empty, but I didn't want to call an ambulance – how do you know when it is *that* bad if you are alone? I managed to drive myself to my doctor's office, whereupon I collapsed again, this time in front of a long line up of people, some of whom thought I was causing a scene to get preferential treatment.

I was – it bloody hurt.

I was grateful the surgery nurse managed to get me on a stretcher and into a treatment room, where my Doctor had a quick feel around and said two words that were to dominate my life for the better part of the next three months.

"Kidney Stones," he said.

Within an hour I had been taken by ambulance to the Emergency Room of the nearest hospital and was on another stretcher lying in a passageway waiting to be examined, suffering the most intense pain I could ever imagine a human could endure. In fact, at one point, I felt a hand gently take mine, while a soothing voice told me everything was going to be fine. I opened my eyes to see a priest next to me and I honestly thought he was about to administer the last rites. To be frank, at that point in my life, it would have been fine with me.

Eventually – it wasn't that long – I saw a doctor who confirmed the first diagnosis and then proceeded to tell me she had had three children and one kidney stone, and would gladly give birth to the kids again rather than experience another kidney stone.

Pumped full of the best pain medication the Canadian healthcare system can provide, I was sent for a CT scan, which revealed three stones, the largest of which was seven millimetres in size – almost the size of a kernel of corn. Now, before you scoff (again) about the fact I am making a deal about something so small, ask anyone who has had a seven millimetre kidney stone how much fun it is and also consider the size of the pipe this thing was trying to pass through.

The next phase in this little debacle saw me meeting the local urologist, who informed me I would stay on the pain medication for a couple of weeks and if the stones didn't pass, I would require laser surgery to destroy them.

They didn't pass, and two weeks later I was back under the careful attention of said urologist who didn't explain the procedure too well in that I thought laser meant they would point something at my right-hand side and press a few buttons to turn those stones to powder.

Simple, right?

Wrong.

They had to thread the laser up my urinary tract and that journey only starts in one place. So under an effective anesthetic I went, and out I came an hour later, minus the stones, but proudly benefitting from what I can only describe as one of man's best-ever inventions: a catheter. Seriously, the genius who invented this contraption really did those of us who have ever needed one a very large favour! An overnight stay was required and although I still hadn't really passed too much fluid, I was relieved of all extraneous equipment and sent home the following lunchtime.

Not for long.

By early evening I was back in some major pain and a call to the urologist resulted in the recommendation I return to the ER to have a new catheter fitted. An hour later, in a packed (and I mean packed!) waiting room, a rather large and very loud nurse called out my name, which focused the whole room's attention in my direction, especially when she asked if I was the guy waiting to have a catheter fitted. Like I said earlier, these things really are an amazing addition to a man's wardrobe, and the pleasure of not having to get up during the night or rush to the washroom is life-enhancing. Yet, I was still in serious pain when I arrived at the urologist's office two days later for a checkup and collapsed in the waiting room surrounded by elderly gentlemen who, rather than offer to help me, continued unabated with their tales of the prostate.

I was taken into hospital again for another CT scan, after which it was revealed that the surgery had not only destroyed my kidney stones, it had also ruptured a fairly significant portion of my urinary tract, causing blood and urine to flood into my kidneys.

Oh, happy days.

So, I went back in for more surgery and the fitting of a stent which remained in place for two weeks, after which my situation improved and I returned to business as usual.

Now, I don't for one minute claim the medical travails of my life can in any way be compared to the horrendous experiences of so many other people out there who suffer from debilitating medical conditions. But I can attest to the fact that even something that seems relatively insignificant – like an ingrown toenail or a seven millimetre kidney stone – can represent adversarial challenges that can really screw us up at times. When we see someone dealing with adversity, it is probably not always wise to make comparisons on the relative scale of the situation – but it makes something like *Running in the Rain* seem pretty tame by comparison, right?

And if someone is suffering, they are suffering.[15]

## Mental Adversity

The second form of adversity I'm keen to address here is mental adversity. This unseen enemy is a cruel beast. Mental adversity comes in many forms, some of which are a direct result of the physical examples described above and some of which are totally independent. The greatest challenges are almost certainly contained within this category and it is the way in which we deal with the mental adversity we face in our lives that can define our

---

[15] Although certain soccer players still push things a bit too far at times.

own personal pathway. The treatment of mental disorders has changed significantly over the last 100 years, with the use of more advanced pharmacological medications, refinements in psychological therapies, insights into the genetic and biological bases of mental illness, and advances in operational diagnosis and classification. And yet, the role of psychosocial stress and the relationship between psychosocial adversity and psychiatric diagnosis remains controversial.

Suicide is a classic outcome of both psychosocial adversity and mental illness – it's basically the inability to overcome mental adversity – and the main culprits have not really changed: loneliness, breakdowns in relationships, chronic pain and ongoing stress are still major risk factors for such deaths. The trauma leading to these outcomes can be acute (e.g. bereavement due to the loss of a loved one), recurrent (e.g. domestic violence) or chronic (e.g. poverty).

From here we can all probably relate to the fact we often feel vulnerable as we face adversity.

But can adversity make us stronger? Well, that's kind of why we are here because *Running in the Rain* is not really a physical challenge (unless we have some rare skin condition); it is about the mind telling us an experience is going to be horrible.

Another compounding factor in understanding mental adversity is the inability of an individual to recognize their own symptoms or the tendency of a third party, qualified or not, to misdiagnose or, even worse, to stereotype someone based on a lack of awareness of their circumstances. Take, for example, someone's breakup with someone who was violent. Even though it may seem like the best outcome, that may not at first be the feelings of the victim.

Possibly one of the most significant advances in the treatment of mental illness has been the recognition of Post-Traumatic Stress Disorder. Military personnel returning from operations are now far more likely to be screened for PTSD than they would have been even 20 years ago, and we only have to go back a couple of decades to realize how badly missed this diagnosis really was. But it isn't just members of the military who suffer from this condition, of course: our Emergency Services personnel are constantly under threat, people experience road accidents or the loss of a loved one and even beloved pets die... all of which can trigger traumatic responses.

One of the more interesting outcomes of studies into this condition is the treatments now available and the knowledge and understanding of psychiatric counsellors. Indeed, over 30 years ago, I was indirectly witness to a significant tragedy while serving in the military. Horrendous though it was, I felt I was coping well but was told to visit the "shrink" for a checkup. We talked about guilt, something I hadn't thought about until he mentioned it and I left wondering if I should actually be feeling it more. Like I said, I was doing okay until I went to that appointment. It took me a while to get over it and I didn't go back for more.

Thankfully, in part at least, people understand better today that human cognition, emotion, and behaviour are complex, interconnected and prey to a variety of influences – e.g. genetics and biology, and psychological, social and cultural forces – whose effects do not always immediately rise to the surface. Psychiatry, at this moment in time, has been compared to biology before Darwin and astronomy before Copernicus and while there have been strong advances in the recognition and treatment of mental distress and disease, mental adversity remains, on the surface, a poor second to its physical cousin.

As with physical adversity, even what might appear to be the most minor of issues can create quite incredible levels of concern – a kind of mental ingrown toenail or kidney stone.

## Emotional Adversity

Most of us desperately need to learn how to have our feelings without letting them overcome us, and this tends to be one of the benefits of increasing emotional maturity – which itself stems from experience and an effective state of mind. Those who don't have that maturity face more difficulties in life.

Value, meanwhile, is defined as "the regard that something is held to deserve." We place value in things like possessions, skills, and, especially, people. But the most important thing we should value, from the perspective of a sound level of emotional maturity, is our self. However, the problem many people face now, and probably more now than ever before, is knowing how to measure our self-worth or value. An ounce of competitiveness in someone's nature creates a feeling of needing to be special and above average to feel good, but of course, *everyone* can't be above average – it doesn't work like that. Where most people seem to miss the point is that they fail to assess themselves and only themselves.

It can be really tough, but it's only going to get tougher if you fail to value yourself enough, and instead of making comparisons with others, it may be better to set your bar up and measure accordingly.[16]

Of course, self-confidence is a very large part of self-value and this ties in with so much of the mental adversity we looked at earlier with regards to the image we may have of ourselves from a physical perspective; a poor self-image has significant negative mental health implications. And, too, our career paths are almost always going to reflect our levels of emotional adversity and self-value. CEOs are fairly unlikely to suffer from a lack of self-confidence or emotional adversity, but at the same time, you could not make an exact comparison with a front-line worker. Some of them are full of confidence.

Lack of personal value can also hurt us financially as it could mean we decline the opportunity to apply for a much better-paid job or

---

[16] For the record, I won the 2018 Mont Tremblant Ironman triathlon – to be precise, I won the "British Male Athlete between the ages of the 55-59 Category." The fact I was the *only* British Male in that category did not deter me from celebrating a fine victory that evening!

promotion. It can hurt us personally, as it can badly affect relationships, or even keep them from getting started altogether.[17]

Emotions are an enduring, ever-present and continual force in our lives. Sometimes painful, they drive us day by day. We take risks because we're excited about new opportunities. We feel pain for what we can't have, and we make sacrifices for things we want. Without a doubt, our emotions direct our thoughts, intentions and actions with authority superior to our rational minds. But when we act on our emotions too soon, we often make decisions we later lament. Our feelings can alter between dangerous extremes. Veer too far one way and you're bordering on rage. Steer too much to the other and you're in a state of exorbitant happiness. When they are strong, our emotions are usually best met with a sense of moderation and rational perspective. This is not to say that we should stop ourselves from celebrating success or the truly finer things in life, but we must handle negative emotions with extreme care.

As we are all aware, negative emotions tend to spiral out of control, especially immediately after they've been triggered. And over time, these sorts of emotions can grow like weeds, slowly conditioning the mind to function on detrimental feelings and dominating daily life. We have probably all met people who seem to be constantly angry or hostile. They weren't born that way. But they allowed certain emotions to stir within them for so long they became inbred feelings arising all too frequently.

Why did this happen? Maybe it derived from physical adversity. Maybe it has something to do with mental or emotional adversity. But more likely all three are combined in some way because when you add it all up so far, it is quite the little cocktail we are putting together here.

---

[17] I was once obsessed with a beautiful girl in my high school class but simply could not pluck up the courage to ask her out on a date. In fact, I couldn't even bring myself to talk to her at the end-of-year dance, even though she seemed to be spending the whole evening looking in my direction. Many years later I met her again, by which time she was married with two children: she told me how much she had liked me and had really wanted me to talk to her that evening... AAAAARGH).

## Social Adversity

How we interact with people is pretty important if we want to be successful, and if we want to be amongst people we like, enjoy the company of others, be popular with our colleagues, families and extended families and get along well with anyone who can contribute gainfully to our personal or professional well-being. Or just to live a smooth life in order to attain peace and quiet... or just peace.

Life is going to be quite lonely without friends by your side, although as an only child I grew up enjoying my own company and still do to this day, despite being very happily married. I have no problem spending long periods of time alone, especially if I am travelling on business. But it's likely you won't advance your career if the people you report to, or work with, don't enjoy being around you, although of course the success of someone in business is dependent on more than popularity.

Another angle on the work component of social adversity relates to the difficult decisions we may have to make with colleagues and subordinates while in a leadership position. While being popular can make your life and work experience more enjoyable, if you allow your team to perform badly rather than deal with poor performance, are you simply focusing on a quiet life to the detriment of your responsibilities as a leader?

I have worked for many leaders who simply refused to allow for poor performance, requiring my colleagues and me to work harder than we felt we needed to on some of our projects.

Did we feel aggrieved?

Probably.

Did our leader feel any social adversity?

I doubt it – they didn't really care about what their subordinates thought, they had a job to do and they got on with it, which, in the long-term made me appreciate and respect their approach.

After my first promotion during my military career, the Warrant Officer in charge of my department called me into his office, congratulated me, and gave me some sound advice: forget your friends. At the time I felt this was a little bit over the top and I did not plan to cut off any of my friendships, even though many of them were now a rank below me. But he was right. Some of my friends decided they would try to take advantage of me. Others were clearly upset I had been promoted ahead of them and one – who I had always thought was a very good friend – didn't even talk to me for six months. However, others who I had never really thought of as close friends reached out, gave sound advice, supported me and went on to become true and loyal friends for many years.

What stuck out for me was the importance of the golden word, "integrity." Using the principle of doing the right thing whether someone could see me or not reminded me that it was more important to execute my duties than it was to focus only on being popular. That principle has always stood me in good stead and many years after my first military promotion I found myself elected president of a performing arts organization. I was in charge of all artistic output, as well as a significant debt. I had to rely heavily on a volunteer Board of Directors, most of whom appeared dormant and not willing to step up and commit to their responsibilities.

I spent the first three months in this position meeting with each director to discuss their thoughts, commitment and drive. Some of them had been with the organization for more than 30 years, but despite this record of service, I felt the need to make a tough call and let most of them go. This almost produced a mutiny, as many felt it was outrageous they would no longer be part of the executive and therefore unable to guide the direction of an organization which had only been going in one direction for several years... down.

The outcome?

My name was dirt, some very aggressive communication came my way, and some regular members of the organization left in disgust. We also lost some sponsors and for several months I wondered if I had made a huge mistake.

But slowly we saw the grass shoots of recovery start to take hold. New people started becoming interested in the organization. The remaining board members started stepping up and brought new people to our table. Our local grants increased alongside our fundraising results and we developed new sponsors who were happy to find out more about what we were doing, as they had lost interest as a result of the previous administration's actions. Within a year we had cleared our debt and shortly after that started reporting a surplus.

But the most interesting component of the whole exercise related to some of the communication I started receiving from some of the board members I had asked to leave, people who had been among my greatest critics. It was extremely reassuring to hear them state that although they had been unhappy with my decision at the time, they now recognized how right I had been. They had become stale and what I had done was in the best interest of the organization. It took courage for those people to reach out to me and I respect them for that. Some didn't connect with me afterward, and I fear they still look at me with disdain, no matter the success we managed to create at the time. In my mind, those people are dealing with some social adversity brought on by their own unwillingness to acknowledge that the decisions were made for the benefit of the organization, rather than for their own self-interest.

Of course, many people struggle with social anxiety through no fault of their own. Some people may feel awkward in social environments and others may fall somewhere on the autism spectrum. Others may appear confident and outgoing people but in reality are introverts. Indeed, anyone who has attended keynote presentations, workshops, talks, or any other type of event at which I may be speaking, would, hopefully, have seen a confident, well-prepared and professional person stand up and talk. But as anyone who knows me well enough will attest, I am naturally introverted and hate "networking" events. I would rather spend an evening in total isolation or talk for an hour to a room of 1,000 guests than make small-talk to a group of strangers... most of whom are trying to sell me something.

Is this a form of social adversity?

To me it absolutely is: although being with large groups of people I don't know very well is at times a professional requirement, it makes me uncomfortable.

But we often attract opposites. Where I would rather keep myself totally to myself in public, my wife and my mother would happily spend an evening chatting to a whole restaurant and getting to know a bunch of complete strangers.

Not me, thank you very much.

## Spiritual Adversity

Faith in some kind of a higher power is generally an advantage in life. That higher power doesn't even have to be a god, though for many people it is, of course. People who believe strongly in the human spirit, the power of community, or something equally important, will often attain a sense of peace many others do not experience. There are a number of references to adversity in the Bible including:

*Joshua 1:9*

*Be strong and courageous; do not be frightened or dismayed, for the Lord, your God is with you wherever you go.*

*Deuteronomy 31:6,8*

*Be strong and bold; have no fear or dread of them, because it is the Lord your God who goes before you. He will be with you; he will not fail you or forsake you.*

Many more biblical passages reference the routes which can be taken to overcome adversity and claim that your god will help and save you in time of adversity.

But spirituality in itself is intended to be a means to an end in the battle to overcome adversity, is it not? We all face times of severe stress when it comes to certain aspects of our lives. Do we not turn to our spirituality to help us when we feel we desperately need it? There is a saying in the military that there are no atheists in a shell scrape [18] when the mortar shells are raining down. But if that's the case, if we all turned to our religions in times of great need wouldn't the atheists all be gone?

I decided to cease any religious affiliation some time ago but would suggest that even atheists need spirituality, albeit in a different form. We look in other directions. I am at peace in my own company, especially when in the open air, maybe on a long bike ride, a long run or just walking in the trails along the rivers near where I live in Ontario. I felt great spiritual adversity when I asked for guidance from God a few years ago and it felt like He was no longer there for me. I had, up to that point, been generally agnostic, but had on occasions felt there had been divine intervention in my life. But that all disappeared, leading me to think deeply about what I wanted. If there was a god, I reasoned, then I didn't need him to help me along. At the end of the day, he isn't going to stop the rain when I look out the window in the morning, so I might as well accept I'm going to get wet and get on with it.

I went on to do a lot of research into atheism and found the most interesting thing about it was the number of people who had felt the same spiritual adversity as I had and who had taken the same route to land, eventually, in a life guided by atheistic thinking. And of course, any of the various forms of adversity we've talked about here will almost certainly at some point challenge a person's strength in their faith – and kudos to those who feel it helps them through it. For many, however, those challenges will often bring the realization that they are on their own, so they had better get on and deal with it.

Is spiritual adversity simply doubt in your god? Not necessarily, and we could spend the whole of this book discussing it, so I'm just going to leave my own and very personal angle on it right there.

---

[18] A shell scrape is a shallow hole a soldier will dig to lie in during combat to obtain some protection from enemy fire; at the same time, it provides a defensive fighting position.

## Financial Adversity

Financial adversity is interesting as it is really quite subjective in its position in the adversity spectrum. As the saying goes, we don't miss what we never had, and many people probably find a reasonable standard of living acceptable. But for those with visions of grandeur, the stakes are higher, and when things go wrong, the losses are way more severe: the bigger you are, the harder you fall. An opulent lifestyle is all well and good when times are bright and shiny, but it might not last forever. And how do we define a financially adverse situation?

Does a gambling addict face financial adversity if he often loses heavily?

Does someone who keeps going bankrupt due to continual investments in poor business ventures – motivated by the drive for expedited financial gain – face financial adversity?

Does the victim of a serious scam face financial adversity?

I'd say the last example is the only true example because the first two are more self-inflicted – rather like my rugby injuries. While individuals in the first two examples do indeed have to overcome the adversity associated with changes in their financial position, their long-term solutions will need some significant work and soul-searching.

## Adversity in General

The aim of this chapter is to outline various components of adversity, to look at different constituents, and to present how people have to confront it in many forms. No one can deny that some people have to endure extremely severe levels of adversity. It hits us in many forms, but it is ultimately the recipient who has to declare how severe it seems to them and what action, if any, they are going to take to master it. No matter the perception associated with it, *any* form of adversity is adversity. Many go through life dealing with it quietly and in a way that will always remain unknown to another living person. And some people are harshly judged when it seems they are making an issue out of something which seems minor or insignificant. Once again, ingrown toenails and kidney stones really hurt, and they can screw up your whole life.

You may feel a bit rough after a bad night, a failed alarm has made you a bit late, your egg broke and the car won't start, but all that is behind you now, so look for some adversity you can overcome to make you feel better.

Look, it's raining, go for a run, because by focusing not on the rain, but on what the rain can do for you, you can become more resilient in the face of adversity. Then consider how the practice of *Running in the Rain* can change your lifestyle in order to help you consistently use a *system* to ensure you overcome your challenges and hit your goals.

# Conclusion

*You can't finish what you don't start, and you should never start what
you're not committed to finish.*

**–Gary Ryan Blair**

One of the best parts of running is finishing. That doesn't mean the whole experience up to that point has been a dreadful nightmare, it means that getting to the end signifies you have accomplished what you set out to do. You should have a few endorphins zipping around your head and you can check it all off as a job well done for the day.

What then? A drink, a good stretch, and a hot shower. And it is during the shower that I always feel the most gratification for being able to run and enjoy a feeling of achievement, no matter the distance or time. If I have been *Running in the Rain*, the process is a little different because everything is soaking wet. My shoes need to be stuffed with paper to dry out and peeling off my wet clothes is a bit more of an effort than usual. But the post-rain run shower, is really something else. The hot water hits my head after a period of cold rain, and the heat of the hot water replenishes my body, the feeling of a truly deep cleansing process washes away not only the rain but the associated dirt and grime from the road or trail on which I ran… they all elevate the experience above the normal. Standing under the hot water reflecting on what I have just accomplished is the most notable part of my day's running experience.

I did not allow the rain to stop me. I took on the adversity laid down in front of me. I challenged it head-on. I did not run slower than usual. I did not reduce my distance. In fact, I used the rain as a tool to overcome adversity on the journey to feeling pretty good. My system was challenged and held firm. I may have worn specific clothes. I may have worn old shoes. I may have needed a thick plastic bag for my phone. So what? I had a system in place that ensured I was out the door and getting on with it. But the most important part of the system was my mindset around *Running in the Rain*: the rain didn't stop me.

If *Running in the Rain* is a metaphor for life, then getting it done, pulling off the wet clothes, and getting into a hot shower is a metaphor for looking back at a good day's work.

During the day you stayed in your zone and you built your Mental Energy pack through effective physical effort. You applied systems to achieve your goals. You focused on the right tasks at the right time. You completed several periods of work, free from distraction. You kept outbound communication to a minimum while managing anything sent your way. You gauged the effort required to get your work done efficiently and ensured you applied yourself in a committed and productive manner. You didn't dwell upon or delay tasks that needed your attention. And you faced up to any adversity that presented itself by taking it on and dealing with it in order to get the job done.

I love being active, being outside, and staying fit. I love the feeling of taking on a task, creating a system, and achieving my goals, both in business and in my personal and social life. In many ways, all the things I have shared through this book come quite naturally to me, but I have also had to work at them. Do I ever feel like NOT *Running in the Rain*? Of course, but that simply makes the post-run shower even more wonderful. And the same applies to business. Do I ever feel like *not* making that sales call or talking to a difficult client? Likewise, the answer is yes, but the beauty of having a *Running in the Rain* mentality is that I know how I will feel when I have gone ahead, made the call, and completed an onerous task.

If you have ever hesitated over aspects of your life you just wish you could move forward and get done, or if you feel you want to be more efficient, functional or productive – or simply be a bit better at doing stuff – then I hope some of what I have shared here encourages you to make changes. These systems are all pretty simple and, I believe, practical, so I urge you to give them a try.

And at the end of the day, we are only really talking about *Running in the Rain*, because when you think about it: *Seriously… how hard can it be?*

# Acknowledgments

*I* often wonder how many readers actually bother to do more than just scan this part of a book or just leave it completely alone. I should probably confess I am guilty of not paying a lot of attention to it, so I hope I am in a very small minority and most people who get this far keep going, for another couple of pages at least.

Writing this book had been at the back of my mind for a few years, and after numerous prompts from some friends and colleagues, I felt I ought to take my own advice, stop messing around, and basically get on with it.

Firstly, a huge thanks to Susan Crossman my editor. I am not someone who takes criticism lightly, but she made it clear none of her comments were personal, they were just in the best interests of the book. Although I did not necessarily agree with everything at first glance, have to admit that on second reading, pretty much everything she said made sense. I am also encouraged that this book has inspired her to start running again and sort out her inbox.

But I would probably not have connected with Susan had it not been for my friends and business associates, Mike and Vickey Gibson, who, after reading the first draft of Chapter 1, gave me the thumbs-up to keep going.

Susan was also gracious enough to recommend Spotlight publishing as a potential partner, and they have assisted with great professionalism in helping to get this book out into the big world.

Other thanks should go to those who also read some initial drafts and provided useful feedback that I was on to something here, so get it done. These include my good friend Tali Bar-Or and my former boss, Tammy Berberick at Crestcom International.

There have been many people who have inspired me over the years, none more so than Sir Rob Fulton, who as Commandant General Royal Marines, provided me with '*top cover*' on numerous occasions. Never has the term '*contagious leadership*' been more appropriate than when I consider the influence he had on my career and my life in general. It was an honour that he so kindly agreed to write the foreword to this book.

There are many others who have played a part in my professional and personal development; too many to share names here, but I'm hoping that if you read this because you know me, then you should take some gratification from the fact that you made a contribution to my life, so thanks.

Finally, the biggest acknowledgments are to the three most important people in my life. My parents, Wendy and Roy Weston, who brought up a son I know they are immensely proud of, and that wouldn't be the case had they not done it right (although I must admit I harbour thoughts of my mum and Susan going head-to-head in a grammar test). And my wife Katie for her encouragement, but more importantly her willingness to just leave me alone to get on with it.

# Notes:

**Chapter 4**

"A 2012 McKinsey study found that": Chui, Micaek, et al. "The Social Economy: Unlocking Value and Productivity Through Social Technologies". McKinsey Global Institute. July 2012. https://www.mckinsey.com/industries/technology–media–and–telecommunications/our–insights/the–social– economy

"Tom Cochran HBR Chief Digital Strategist to Barack Obama, White House and Department of State": Cochran, Tom. "Email Is Not Free." Harvard Business Review, April 8, 2013. http://blogs.hbr.org/2013/04/email–is–not–free/.

"The Truth About Digital Distraction in the Workplace": Macdonell, Robby, CEO, RescueTime, et al. "HR Daily Advisor" August 7, 2018. https://hrdailyadvisor.blr.com/2018/08/07/truth–digital–distraction–workplace/

"A 4–Day Workweek? A Test Run Shows a Surprising Result": Graham-McLay, Charlotte. *The New York Times* July 19, 2018. https://www.nytimes.com/2018/07/19/world/asia/four–day–workweek–new–zealand.html

"Udemy 2018 Workplace Distraction Report": https://research.udemy.com/research_report/udemy–depth–2018–workplace–distraction–report/

"The Cost of Interrupted Work: More Speed and Stress": Mark, Gloria. Department of Informatics, University of California, Irvine. Gudith, Daniela, and Kloche, Ulrich. Institute of Psychology, Humboldt University, Berlin. https://www.ics.uci.edu/~gmark/chi08–mark.pdf

Anders Ericsson was a leading academic researcher from Florida State University. More about his career in the area of human performance can be found at: https://psy.fsu.edu/imagenews/imagenews.php?newsfile=imagenews6_19_20.php

## Chapter 7

"Effect of Anticipation During Unknown or Unexpected Exercise Duration on Rating Perceived Exertion, Affect and Physiological Function": Baden, D. A., T. L. McLean, R. Tucker, T. D. Noakes, and A. St. Clair Gibson. British Journal of Sports Medicine 39, no. 10 (October 2005): 742– 746.

## Chapter 8

"Solving the Procrastination Puzzle: A Concise Guide to Strategies for Change": Pychyl, Timothy A. Penguin Books.

# About Paul Weston

*P*aul Weston grew up in York-shire, England, and after a youth absorbed in music and sport, at age 16, joined the Royal Marines Band Service. Over the next 26 years, his duties took him around the globe, and on completion of his military career, he immigrated to Canada where he joined the North American corporate world consulting in Leadership Development and Sales. He also coaches executives, corporations and individuals in Time Freedom techniques.

A multiple Ironman triathlete and international duathlete, his mantra is not to find time to do things but to plan them. His Energy Zone theory adopts the principle that too much of our effort is wasted on pointless distractions, and too many people make terrible excuses rather than getting on with life.

Find out more about working with
Paul Weston and his team at www.andrewjane.com

Like what you have read?
We welcome reviews

Made in the USA
Middletown, DE
28 March 2022

63290937R00099